CONTENTS

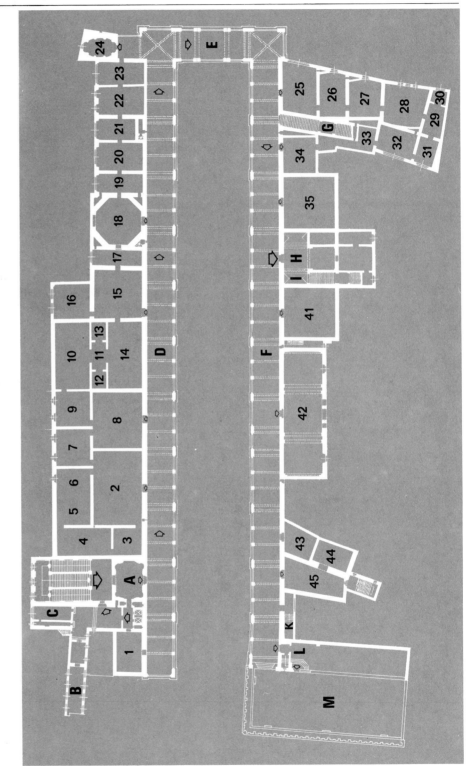

© 1971 SCALA *
Istituto Fotografico Editoriale, Firenze
Color photographs: SCALA, Florence
Layout: Leone Sbrana
Translation: Rowena Fajardo
Produced by SCALA, Istituto Fotografico Editoriale
Printed in Italy by
Officine Grafiche Firenze, 1981

On cover:
Botticelli: portrait of unknown man
Zoffany: tribune

The Uffizi

In 1560, when construction of the Uffizi began, the political status of Florence had recently changed. She had conquered the Republic of Siena, quite suddenly, between 1554 and 1555, and Duke Cosimo had thus made himself ruler of a large regional state of which Florence (which up to then had been simply a city-state) became the capital. In the year 1560, after a ceremonial entry into Siena, Cosimo proceeded to Roma to be received by Pope Pius IV, who planned to make him King of Tuscany. His son Francesco wrote to him on that occasion: "I know your Excellency will have had his way with regard to antiquities, and will have found more than enough to decorate the Camerino, for you write that you mean to despoil Rome of these things. I look forward to seeing them..." The sculptures he was referring to are probably now in the Gallery, but at that time Cosimo's only intention with regard to the Uffizi was to create an administrative center conveniently near to the Palazzo Vecchio, the seat of government. It was to house the offices (hence the name Uffizi) or magistracies (and the very first name of the palace was in fact "i Magistrati").

Encouraged by his successes, Cosimo aimed at new glory by making of Florence a city of impressive monuments, and for the arts it was a time of vigorous activity. Benvenuto Cellini and Bartolomeo Ammannati competed for the fountain in the Piazza Signoria; Ammannati also began the construction of the grand courtyard of Palazzo Pitti; Giambologna was at work on sculpture for the Medici court; and the Palazzo Vecchio was being redecorated as a royal residence. The new Uffizi Palace was Vasari's masterpiece, striking in perspective, with its rows of regularly placed windows and the long open galleries on either side, formal and yet not heavy. He used systematically throughout the Tuscan order (with architraves instead of arches over the supporting columns) and the traditionally Florentine contrast of pietra serena, the local grey stone, on white plaster.

The building stretches from the Palazzo Vecchio to the Arno, around three sides of a long courtyard. Its construction posed difficult technical problems, as Vasari himself writes: "I have never built anything more difficult nor more dangerous, since its foundations are over the river, almost in the air". It took in fact twenty years, being finished by Buontalenti after Vasari's death; but in 1565 when Francesco dei Medici married Joanna of Austria, the daughter of the Emperor, the unique corridor which leads from the Uffizi over archways and other buildings, all the way across the Arno to the Pitti Palace and the Boboli gardens, was built in only five months.

We do not know exactly for what reason Francesco I, when he succeeded Cosimo, decided (beginning in 1581) to make the upper loggia of the Uffizi into a museum. He might have felt that the light and airy corridors, the picture-like views framed by the architectural spaces, were asking for works of art to complete them. Or he may simply have wanted, eccentric that he was, and impatient with the problems of government, to create a private refuge where he could enjoy his artistic and scientific hobbies and remain at the same time in close contact with his political center. There is in fact an overpass which joins the Uffizi and the Palazzo Vecchio; and coming from Palazzo Pitti along the corridor — as if by one of the aerial roads dreamed of by Leonardo — Francesco could reach a secret window looking into the Palazzo Vecchio, and watch unseen over the proceedings at the hearings. "Thus it was his habit to linger often in this palace..." (Bocchi, 1591). In any case, the collections made by the Medici were by now in need of adequate housing, and to give them a place near the Palazzo Vec-

▲
View of the third Corridor

◄
Ceiling of the first Corridor of the Uffizi Gallery

The splendor of the Uffizi Gallery is not only in the works it contains, but also in the building itself. Its three corridors, flooded with light from their great windows, are already a magnificent spectacle. The eighteenth century paving of marble blocks in the eastern corridor may be colder in tone, but in the southern and western corridors the original red brick floors match the warm tones of the frescoed vaults. The colorful overall effect is completed by the tapestries and the statues, whose bases, as tests reveal, were once painted. We find here the continuation of the lively decorative style of Vasari's rooms in the Palazzo Vecchio. It is carried even further in the grotesques of the ceilings on the east side (1581). From the south end the views over the Arno and up the Uffizi courtyard to the Palazzo Vecchio are magnificent; while the continuation of the Gallery in the corridor leading across the Ponte Vecchio to Palazzo Pitti gives us a glimpse of the amazing unitary development of the ancient museums of Florence.

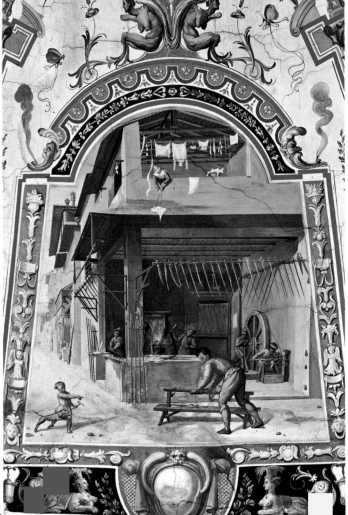

Poccetti: Maker of Swords

7

chio, in the heart of Florence, meant to make them an integral part of the city's image, the symbol of her cultural prestige.

We can reconstruct from records the arrangement of the earliest Gallery, nearly four centuries ago. Part of it has remained to this day, in spite of subsequent changes. On the east side, above the present entrance, the first suite of rooms we enter today did not exist because it was part of the Medici Theater, also founded by Francesco (1586), where marvelous spectacles were held, with scenery by Buontalenti. The foyer of the Theater is still there, beside the present Drawings and Prints Room, with fine entrance doors surmounted by Giambologna's bust of Francesco. Coming from Palazzo Vecchio one entered the eastern corridor, decorated with fine grotesques (1581, paintings by Allori, Bizzelli, etc., usually attributed to Poccetti), where antique and contemporary sculpture, portraits of the Medici and of famous men in various fields, and artist's self-portraits were exhibited. Nearer to the river began a sequence of small rooms, still existing today, outstanding among which was the Tribune.

The Tribune (1584; designed by Buontalenti), is octagonal in shape, and had complex cosmological meaning, still decipherable. On the lantern above the dome is a weathervane connecting on the inside to an arrow which points in the direction of the wind, an obvious reference to Air. The mother-of-pearl inlay lining the dome and the blue of the drum refer to Water, the red covering of the walls to Fire, and the splendid floor in pietra serena, with green as its basic tone, to the Earth. But as well as the four elements the Tribune symbolized the Medici (the family's armorial bearings are painted on the ribs) and the virtues of the Grand Duke (represented as the Labors of Hercules in silver statuettes by Giambologna which have since been lost). There are also various other allusions now of little significance. Thus in Heikamp's words, "the glory of the Prince is depicted, surrounded by cosmological symbols, and his power is a part of the order imposed by God on the world". The Tribune, however, was also a temple of all the arts. On the walls were crowded some thirty classical paintings: five by Raphael, six by Andrea del Sarto, two by Pontormo, one by Beccafumi and one by Piero di Cosimo. But other artists too, such as the contemporary Ligozzi and the Flemish Civetta, were represented. At eye level an ebony shelf ran round the room, with drawers full of medals and valuable small objects; on the shelf stood statuettes, "in-

struments", mounds of trinkets. At intervals all around were bronze figures by Giambologna and others mounted on black consoles bordered in gold (of which one survives). Below the shelf hung more "pictures... bas-reliefs... damascened knives... scabbards with precious jewels". On a painted plinth (by Ligozzi), which has disappeared and been replaced by a Neo-Classical one, were many sorts of birds, fish, waters, plants, stones, shells and other things". In the center of the room, like a reproduction of the Tribune itself on a smaller scale, stood a cabinet in the form of a little octagonal temple (called a Studiolo) designed by Buontalenti, in ebony and gold and precious stones, filled with medals and jewels. Its doors, decorated by Giambologna with bas-reliefs in gold and amethyst and jasper illustrating the deeds of Francesco I are now in the Silver Museum at Palazzo Pitti. The Studiolo itself, now vanished, has been replaced by a large table in pietre dure, patterned all over, which took sixteen years to make (1633-1649). A second cabinet, placed in the niche opposite the entrance, and famous antique statues such as the Medici Venus, were added later to the decoration of the Tribune. Changes were occasionally made also in the pictures exhibited, but these were always among the most important.

Extremely luxurious, of a somewhat heavy taste but based on scholarly criteria, the Tribune soon became famous, and it had a decisive influence on the newborn discipline of museum architecture. It embodied principles which today are open to doubt but which for a long time prevailed: the sumptuous central room to which other rooms relate; lighting not from winodws at eye-level but from above (and from windows "of oriental glass that they should give a purer light"), thus creating an atmosphere more isolated from the outside world; full use of wall space to show several tiers of paintings, emphasizing the size and value of the collection; a general impression of magnificence to which each work contributes its part. A painting (c. 1775) by Zoffany in the English royal collection (it was Queen Charlotte who sent the artist to Florence especially to paint it) shows us the Tribune as it was at that time, admired by countless visitors on their "grand tour" of Europe, crammed with works of all kinds, crowded with enthusiastic art-lovers. The Tribune has recently (1970) been restored, as far as is possible, to its original state. There can now be seen some of the same paintings as were there in 1589 (when the first inventory was made) or in the years following.

Next to the Tribune is another small room (also restored in 1970) where originally scientific instruments were exhibited and can still be seen pictured in the ceiling frescoes and where later various small curiosities as well as the disturbing antique sculpture of the Hermaphrodite (acquired in Rome in 1669) were placed. In the rooms beyond the Tribune on the other side—also decorated with frescoes alluding to their contents—were antique and modern weapons from every country (with armorers' workshops below); and at the end of the row the Gabinetto di Madama where the antique bronzes, "idols" as they were called, were kept. This was redecorated by Zanobi del Rosso in the late eighteenth century and is now the Miniature Room.

The west side of the Uffizi was not originally a museum, but a series of workshops for the minor arts and the Fonderia or Farmacia where perfumes were distilled, and poisons, antidotes and allegedly miraculous medicines for presenting to distinguished guests were prepared. The Museum was thus encyclopedic, universal, in keeping with the spirit of the times. Art (in the broad sense of human activity which transforms nature) was shown in all its stages and branches, from conception to perfection. History was represented by the busts of figures of antiquity, the medals, the contemporary portraits and self-portraits; geography by objects from all the world. On the west side also, as well as the continuation of Vasari's corridor, was the entrance to the Gallery from the courtyard (with a stairway by Buontalenti, reopened in 1967 by the architect Nello Bemporad). At the end of this wing is the terrace above the Loggia of Orcagna, where originally was a hanging garden with a fountain by Giambologna.

It is worth quoting here a few sentences from an early description of the Gallery, that of F. Pigafetta (1600): "The so-called Uffizi then, new buildings of subtle architecture... where below is carried on the business of the city and cases are heard and notaries write. Above, on the left, is the Gallery, so-called by a French term, in which are gathered together innumerable things, singular and marvelous... (As for the historical portraits)... into this most select company are received only the faces of the great and famous. On the floor at the sides, are arranged the marble statues... the best made... which have remained to us from the ancients, besides the modern ones of Buonarroti and of others which equal those. The Tribune... seems a celestial dwelling, with its starry brilliance

(etc.)... Above the Offices on the right side the rooms are assigned to the various crafts of goldsmiths, watch-makers, carvers of rock crystals, who polish stones and various jewels (etc.)... At the end of this Gallery, above the roof of the Loggia, spreads the garden planted with evergreen trees and flowers... where every day (the young Medici) go late in the afternoon to listen to the music (played in the square by bands)...".

Right up to 1737, when the last of the Grand Dukes, Gian Gastone, died, the Medici continued to add to the Gallery. They also, a couple of centuries before any other rulers, allowed it to be visited on request, at least by people of certain standing. In 1631, when the wife of Ferdinando II, Vittoria della Rovere, inherited Urbino, about sixty splendid paintings came to join the collection, among them the diptych by Piero della Francesca with the portraits of Federico di Montefeltro and Battista Sforza, some Raphaels, several Titians (the portraits of the Duke and Duchess of Urbino, the Venus called of Urbino, the Magdalen, and the Madonna of Mercy and the Englishman now in the Pitti), and works by Palma, Bassano and Barocci. It was Ferdinando II who had completed the frescoes in the southern and western corridors, which were dedicated to the glories of Florence. The work was directed by the librarian Count Ferdinando del Maestro, who supplied the subjects. In the meantime the Grand Duke's brother, the cultivated Cardinal Leopoldo, was building up his own collection, which at his death in 1675 was added to the rest of the Medici collections; to him the Uffizi owes possession of excellent works by Pontormo (Portrait of Francesco Ajolle), Bronzino (Portrait of a Gentleman), Titian (Knight of Malta), Dosso (Witchcraft), Sebastiano del Piombo (Death of Adonis), Paris Bordone (Portrait of a Man), Savoldo (Transfiguration), Moroni (Portrait of Antonio Pantera), Veronese (Martyrdom of St. Justina and Holy Family with St. Barbara), Tintoretto (portraits), Bassano, Palma the Younger and Lys.

There is in the Uffizi a very fine portrait of the distinguished Cardinal himself painted by Baciccio. The Gallery is also indebted to the Cardinal for two of its basic collections: that of the drawings by ancient and contemporary masters, which was put in order by the art historian Baldinucci and brought to the Uffizi in 1700, forming the nucleus of the present collection of Drawings and Prints, and that of the self-portraits of painters from every country. In 1681, to properly display this unique collection, Cosimo III had a new room

Botticelli: Sketch for Pallas

The "Cabinet" of Drawings and Prints of the Uffizi Gallery began with the collection of Cardinal Leopoldo dei Medici; when he died (1675) Cosimo III had the material ordered in 100 volumes by the art historian F. Baldinucci, whose own collection of drawings went, however, in 1806 to the Louvre.

Cosimo III then had the drawings and prints taken from Palazzo Pitti to the Uffizi, and at that time 47000 drawings were discarded! In 1778 P. Leopoldo acquired from the Gaddi gallery more ancient drawings and prints, and others from the Casa Michelozzi, from the Mariette family and from the painter Hugford.

A small room adjacent to the Tribune was arranged to house the drawings; but in 1854 they were moved to three rooms in the eastern corridor near the Loggia of Orcagna, and in 1886 displayed also in Vasari's corridor, starting with the two rooms at the foot of the stairs and in the stretch along the Lungarno Archibusieri (prints), and then in the part toward the Ponte Vecchio (drawings).

1725 drawings were thus exhibited, but this arrangement ceased in 1882. In the meantime two volumes of architectural drawings (Buontalenti, Pietro da Cortona, Ciro Ferri) were acquired in 1858; in 1866 12461 drawings were left to the Gallery by the sculptor E. Santarelli, while the Torrigiani legacy of 1865 added the complete works of Bartolozzi to the prints.

A thousand architectural drawings left by G. Martelli were added in 1876; in 1881 44 landscape drawings by Poelenburg were acquired; in 1888 71 views of Tuscany by Buci, etc. In 1888 a general inventory of the drawings was completed; it comprised 1700 Italian and foreign artists from the fourteenth century onwards.

By 1937 the figure had reached more than 50,000 drawings and 60,000 prints.

The "Cabinet" of Drawings and Prints, now on the second floor of the Uffizi where the Medici Theater once was, has recently been excellently rearranged with the help on the architectural side of E. Detti (1960). The first room is set aside for exhibitions of high cultural standard, open to the public; and after it come study rooms with photo archive and library, where with an introduction to the director prints and drawings may be examined on request.

◀
Leonardo: Age and Youth
▶
Michelangelo: Madonna and Child

prepared (the present Tintoretto Room), where a statue of Leopoldo was also placed. Unfortunately the Baroque decoration of this room was destroyed late in the last century as a result of a tendency to alterations with no regard for tradition which in modern times has caused confusion and even harm in the museums of Florence.

Cosimo III, the pious Grand Duke who reigned the half century from 1670 to 1723, was also a collector (travelling in Europe in his youth he bought paintings by English and Dutch artists), and added to the Gallery. He created on the west side, opposite the Tribune, a parallel complex of rooms which included the Self-Portraits Room, the Vestibule (1704) at the top of Buontalenti's stairway, adorned with archeological pieces, and a room for the medal collection (now the Rubens Room) which by then consisted of thirty thousand pieces (Cosimo himself had acquired thirteen thousand in a single purchase).

From the Pitti Palace and the Boboli Gardens other statues were brought to the Uffizi; Cosimo brought from Rome three outstanding classical sculptures (the Medici Venus, the Knife-Sharpener, and the Wrestlers). The sculptor Ercole Ferrata supervised their transportation to Florence, where he became the first official restorer for the Gallery, followed by Giuseppe Piemontini and Francesco Franchi. Prince Ferdinando, who was Cosimo's son but did not live to suceed him, was also distinguished as a collector of paintings of unbiased and modern taste; from him the Uffizi inherited, for example, the Madonna of the Harpies by Andrea del Sarto, the Madonna of the Long Neck by Parmigianino, the Portrait of a Old Man by Rembrandt, and Fair at Poggio a Caiano by Crespi. He was the patron of Crespi, as also of Magnasco and the two Ricci, Sebastiano and Marco, who also came to Florence.

In 1737, the Medici family having died out, Tuscany passed into the hands of Francis of Lorraine, the husband of Maria Theresa of Austria. But a famous pact drawn up by the last member of the family, the Palatine Electress Anna Maria Ludovica, stipulated with regard to the art treasures: "nothing that is for the adornment of the state, of benefit to the public, and an attraction to the curiosity of foreigners, shall be transported or taken away from the capital and state of the Grand Duchy". This saved the Uffizi, to which obviously all three conditions applied, from the danger of having its works of art removed to Vienna, and in fact made the collections the inalienable heritage of the city of Florence. It is well to remember, despite recent interpretations justifying the removal of works to Rome and elsewhere on the grounds that the "State" was enlarged with the unification of Italy, that in the will of Anna Maria Ludovica (1743) it is specifically stated that these things "must all, always and for ever be kept in this city of Florence".

The Lorraine dynasty, in any case, were to reveal themselves to be excellent rulers, motivated by reformist ideals of good government, indeed in the vanguard among the European princes in the Enlightenment period. Although they had not the taste and the zeal in support of the arts inborn in even the worst rulers among the Medici, they cared scrupulously for the city's artistic heritage, and for the Uffizi in particular. By the end of the eighteenth century they had completely rearranged its collections according to the ideas of the new "museology", and had also continued to add to them. Of their activity clear traces remain.

The entrance was moved to its present place in the east wing, with a broad stairway leading up to a graceful vestibule by Zanobi del Rosso (previously the entrance to the Medici Theater); the Vestibule is dominated by a bust of Pietro Leopoldo (1790), a very active reformer who left his mark on the Uffizi also. By 1779 the Gallery possessed ninety antique statues and seventy busts, eleven hundred paintings, 162 volumes of drawings, four thousand gems, fourteen thousand antique medals, plus bronzes, miniatures, pieces of majolica, Roman inscriptions, and Etruscan objects. The dominant passion of the century was archeology, and this area was built up by the purchase of the Galluzzi Etruscan Museum at Volterra and the Buccelli Museum, also Etruscan, at Montepulciano. The group of Niobe and her Children had been brought to Florence from the Villa Medici in Rome and set up in a splendid new room built specially for it in the west wing (1780), designed in Neo-Classical style by Gaspare Paoletti and decorated with stuccos by Grato Albertolli. Acquisitions were made also for the collections of modern medals and coins (Orsini Room), and drawings and prints (from the remains of the Gaddi Gallery and from the Casa Michelozzi).

But the picture gallery had also grown considerably, and had begun to give space to so-called "primitives", i.e. painters up to the end of the fifteenth century. Botticelli made his appearance, and Signorelli, Mantegna, Piero della Francesca, Fra Angelico, Filippo Lippi; and from further back still the "very curious" Thebaid of Starnina,

12

Simone Martini and even two "Greek style" Madonnas. Works were brought to the Gallery from villas and properties of the Grand Duchy — in 1794 Leonardo's Adoration of the Magi came from Castello — while others were acquired from religious orders (many of which were about to be suppressed); these included the Deposition by Andrea del Sarto (later exchanged — 1795 — for the Madonna of the Harpies from the Pitti), Barocci's Madonna of the People from the Pieve of Arezzo, Sodoma's St. Sebastian from Siena (transferred in 1928 to the Pitti Palace). With the suppression of the religious orders the Uffizi gained the Tabernacle of the Linaioli by Fra Angelico (now in the Museum of San Marco) and Albertinelli's Visitation. In the last years of the dynasy, between the departure of Pietro Leopoldo for Vienna when he was made Emperor (1790) and the arrival of the French revolutionary troops (1796), Pietro Leopoldo's successor, Ferdinando III, continued to add to the paintings. A shrewd exchange with Vienna in 1793 brought to the Uffizi Dürer's Adoration of the Magi, one of his most important works, Titian's Flora, Palma the Elder's Madonna and Child with Saints, Annibale Caracci's Man with an Ape and the Bacchanal of the school of Rubens, plus other works which later went to the Pitti. Also in 1793 a room was set up in the Uffizi for French paintings, bought at that period in Paris or found in the grand ducal palaces in Florence: the Portrait of Fouquet by Philippe de Champagne, the spectacular Seaport at Sunset by Claude Lorrain, Vouet's Annunciation, and works by Lebrun, Boucher and others. In 1795 paintings were exchanged with the Academy of Fine Arts, by which the Uffizi acquired the St. James of Andrea del Sarto and the two Miracles of St. Zenobius by Ridolfo del Ghirlandaio (now back in the Academy storerooms); and two rooms were arranged for the Venetian school, where fine paintings by artists from Giovanni Bellini and Giorgione to Tintoretto and Veronese, several of which had formerly been in the Villa of Poggio Imperiale, were exhibited. By 1798 the Gallery had become widely representative, comprising, besides the collections already mentioned, many sixteenth century and Baroque works. Errors had been made as well, however; the Medici Armory was almost completely sold off and removed from the Gallery, and the majolica collection was much reduced. Two of Paolo Uccello's Battles were sold after 1784; one went to the Louvre and one to the National Gallery in London. The scientific instruments, on the other hand were transferred between 1771 and 1775 from the Uffizi to the new Natural History Museum (the Specola). On the 12th of August, 1762, a dangerous fire broke out in the Gallery, raging through the west wing from the Loggia to Via Lambertesca, and although fortunately there were not many works there to destroy (nine portraits, six statues and some busts were lost, and the Boar, Bandinelli's copy of Lacoon, and Sansovino's Bacchus were damaged) it ruined twelve of the painted ceilings. These were later repainted (by Giuseppe del Moro, Giuliano Traballesi and Giuseppe Terreni). The fire was caused by the carelessness of the custodian Giuseppe Bianchi, a rather venal character to whom, however, we owe the first detailed guide to the Uffizi (1759). But much more scientific accounts had already been given of the individual sections of the Gallery. One of the first to catalogue the medals and "antiquities" was the Englishman Fitton (1655-56) while Abbot Noris (later Cardinal) continued to work on the medals (1689). A. F. Gori commented on the ancient inscriptions and Etruscan material, while in 1731 the first volume of an imposing ten-volume work, the Florentine Museum, was published (the last came out in 1762). Then came Antonio and Raimondo Cocchi, who catalogued (1761) the medals of the Popes and reorganized the entire Medal Room with the collaboration of the Austrian expert G. Eckel. In 1779 Bencivenni-Pelli published the first historical study of the Museum and the Medici collections, and his collaborator, Abbot Luigi Lanzi, edited a first practical guide to the newly arranged Gallery (which was soon followed by others in various languages, one even in Swedish). In the meantime the Uffizi had been given an official organization; in 1796 the first director was appointed, regulations regarding employees, copyists and visitors were drawn up, an archive was established, and the Royal Guard entrusted with the protection of the Museum both inside and out. In 1795 plaques with the names of the artists were for the first time attached to the paintings, for the guidance of the untrained public.

With regard to this innovation the director Puccini, who had succeeded (1793) Bencivenni-Pelli, commented with great good sense: "Works of art ought to be appreciated for their quality only. But experience teaches us that the name of the artist increases their worth to the public, because many judge the arts from what they have heard or read, few from a full knowledge of what makes them beautiful. An unsuccesful painting, which history

14

One should remember that the Uffizi was originally thought of not as a picture gallery, but as a museum with particular emphasis on a collection of ancient sculpture. Busts and statues are still on display starting at the stairway, and are to be seen in profusion, together with sarcophagi, in each of the three corridors. It is impossible to enumerate all the works here, and one must limit oneself to describing a few of the most important pieces.

In Sala 1, there are, among other archeological finds, two Roman copies of the *Doryphus* of Polyclitus.

The *Medici Venus*, in the Tribune (see introduction) is the most famous of all classical statues in Florence. Louis XIV ordered a bronze copy for himself, visiting Englishmen in the 18th century kissed her hand, Burkhardt called her "one of the greatest delights that Italy has to offer", and Napoleon had her confiscated and sent to the Louvre. She was only returned to Florence in 1815 when Napoleon was defeated. How and where the statue was discovered is not known; our first record of it is in 1638 at the Villa Medici in Rome, at which time Cosimo III had it sent to Florence, fearing that it might prove too provocative for Rome's young art students. The figure seems to derive from the school of Praxiteles of the third century B.C.; the soft modeling and the humanity of the figure, as well as the delicate harmony, all seem Praxitelean. Also in the Tribune is the *Apollino* modeled on the *Apollo* of Praxiteles mentioned (fourth century) by Lucian; the *Dancing Faun*, copy of a Hellenistic original; the group of the *Wrestlers* taken from an original of the School of Pergamum. Here too is the moving and realistic *Knife Sharpener*, kneeling as he awaits orders from Apollo to flay Marsyas. He is a Scythian from southern Russia, one of the slaves in ancient Athens who were employed as executioners. This work is the only direct copy of a work of the Pergamum School in existence; it has been judged a "magnificent copy" or perhaps even the original itself.

In Saletta 17 there is the sensual sleeping *Hermaphrodite*, a Hellenistic copy of the second century B.C. Here too, one finds the charming figures of *Cupid and Psyche*, another Hellenistic work.

◀
Roman bust of a Lady
◀
Bust of Nero
◀
Tribune of Buontalenti
▶
Medici Venus

Filidauro Rossi: Drawing of Vestibule,
Third Corridor, as it Appeared in the 18th
Century

Vestibule, Third Corridor, with *Wild Boar*,
Roman copy of a Greek bronze

16

Veduta degli Ufizj, o sia Curia Fiorentina presa dalla Loggia presso Arno.

125

TXX.

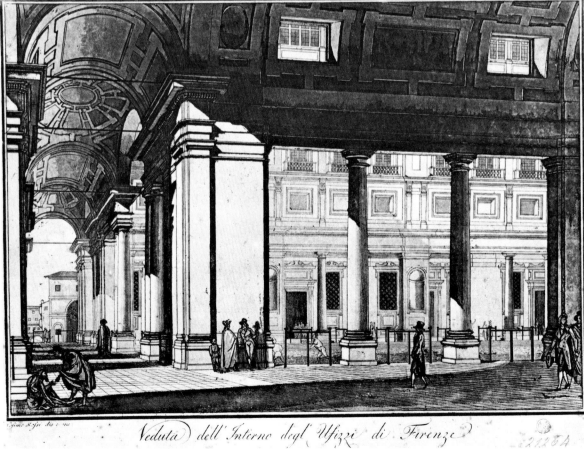

Veduta dell'Interno degl'Ufizzi di Firenze

18

assures us is by the hand of a great master, is preferred to another which is excellent but of uncertain attribution or perhaps by one of his pupils... On this principle I believe that without the paintings in the Royal Gallery improving a whit, they would gain much in the opinion of the world if, all necessary care being taken, the names were attached...".

In 1796 General Bonaparte as he passed through Florence saw this splendid modern gallery, but the fact it was public property and such an integral part of the city itself saved it from the requisitioning by the French to which royal possessions at the Pitti Palace were subjected. A dignified appeal to the Directory by Puccini had been listened to, and only the Medici Venus was subsequently transferred by the Emperor to the Louvre. The statue was returned with the Restoration, but the new era was not to be an entirely favorable one for the Uffizi, in part for the lack of clear overall planning. The last of the Lorraine dynasty showed a preference for their private gallery in the Pitti. From the Uffizi were removed first the Egyptian Museum, then the Gallery of Modern Art, then a collection of paintings which went to Lucca. The National Museum established in the Bargello (1864) on the unification of Italy took the Renaissance sculpture and the minor arts as well, and other works went to the Fra Angelico Museum at San Marco, the Medici Museum, the Horne Museum, and elsewhere. Paintings were sent from the storerooms to adorn government buildings, some at a great distance (even embassies outside Europe), the sets of Medici tapestries were divided up for the same purpose, and thus the collection to some degree lost its integrity as a unique and splendid heritage. And yet it would have been possible to create one great universal museum — along the lines of those which were taking shape at the same time elsewhere in Europe — by extending the Gallery to all the rest of the building instead of bringing in (1852) the State Archive, which occupies four hundred rooms. The once famous Medici Theater, on the other hand, was destroyed (1890) to make way for the first rooms to the east.

Certainly suppression of the religious orders brought to the Uffizi Gallery many outstanding masterpieces of Florentine art formerly scattered throughout the city (and in 1919, with the collection from Santa Maria Nuova, the magnificent triptych by Van der Goes also came to the Uffizi). But there was no definite plan for acquisitions — and prices at the time were low — carefully worked out to fill the gaps in the collections of works from other parts of Italy and from abroad; some paintings were bought, but not many. And the Museum was not equipped technically and scientifically to the degree that comparable institutions in other countries were. The basic mistakes were in allowing specific collections to be moved away to separate museums, often poorly run, and including the Uffizi under a general territorial administration thus depriving it of its fundamental autonomy and preeminence.

The Gallery as a whole is still splendid and distinguished in its field, but it could have been much more so; ranking even higher it would have done much for Italian prestige. However, a reversal of the trend is finally in sight in the plan for a "greater Uffizi" (minus the State Archive, which is now in need of larger premises), drawn up by the architect Nello Bemporad, and in the work in progress in the present Gallery, where the basic collection will remain. It is essential to continue with the renovation of the rooms, broken off after the creation (1956) of some adequately modern ones, and to re-open at long last, all of Vasari's Corridor for the exhibition, until the new Uffizi is ready, of at least a few hundred of the works (at the beginning of the century 2395, in 1952 down to five hundred) now stored away, especially seventeenth and eighteenth-century paintings, self-portraits, and historical portraits. Work must be done — and in fact work is already being done — on restoration, rearrangement, equipment, in short on providing for all the needs of a gallery of such importance, visited by so many people from all over the world. In 1965 a committee of experts valued the Uffizi collections at 600 million dollars (400 billion lire), plus 7 billion lire (11 million dollars) for the building. The number of visitors has increased from 105,000 in 1949 to 761,000 in 1970, making the Uffizi by far the most visited gallery in Italy. Since 1970 there has been an education department which has been very successful with the young students. Our age of technological miracle cannot let pass the opportunity to create a modern Uffizi, to prove itself no less worthy to go down in history with credit than the Medici and House of Lorraine founders.

LUCIANO BERTI

◀Bacchiacca: Tapestry of the Seasons, detail March

Room of the Niobe

The tapestries on display in the corridors of the Uffizi form a unique collection, representing as they do the complete production of the Medicean factories, the most important in Italy, for almost two centuries (c. 1546-1737). There are also splendid pieces from abroad, pieces brought by the Flemish who then taught their art to the Italians. It was Grand Duke Cosimo I who founded the factory in 1545 (it was located on Via degli Arazzieri or street of the Tapestry Workers) under the direction of the well known Flemish weavers Giovanni Van Roost and Nicola Karcher. There was a wide variety of subjects ranging from scenes from the Bible to contemporary events and personages, such as the splendid *Revels at the Court of Catherine de' Medici and Henry II of France*, which we find

in the first corridor. This work is said to be from a cartoon by François Quesnel and was woven in Brussels in the sixteenth century.

Among the most famous of the tapestries are the *Grotesque* on a gold background, designed to serve as chair backs and the *Months of the Year*, all from cartoons by Francesco Ubertini, who was called Il Bachiacca, and woven in Florence (1549-1553) by Roost and Karcher. These are extremely rich in design and color as well as exquisite fantasy in the decorative motifs of festoons, figures, masks, animals, etc. Also in the first corridor are several scenes of *Hunting at Poggio a Caiano* (formerly in the famous Medici villa of that name: 1567-1576) designed by Stradano and executed by Benedetto Squilli.

In the third corridor is a colorful

(despite the subject) series of the *Passion of Christ* from cartoons by Alessandro Allori and Cigoli, woven by Guasparri Papini. The design and execution of this series took place between 1591 and 1609. The other two series *Battle Scenes* and *Stories from the Life of Jacob*, are Flemish and were woven in Brussels in the sixteenth century.

In the foyer of the stairway designed by Buontalenti is a superb tapestry telling the *Stories of Phaeton*. This work is dated in 1617. Richly embroidered curtains, hangings and tapestries decorate other parts of the gallery. Especially elegant is the *Sala of Niobe*, designed to house the famous group of statues of Niobe and her *Children*, Roman copies of Hellenistic originals of the second or third century.

21

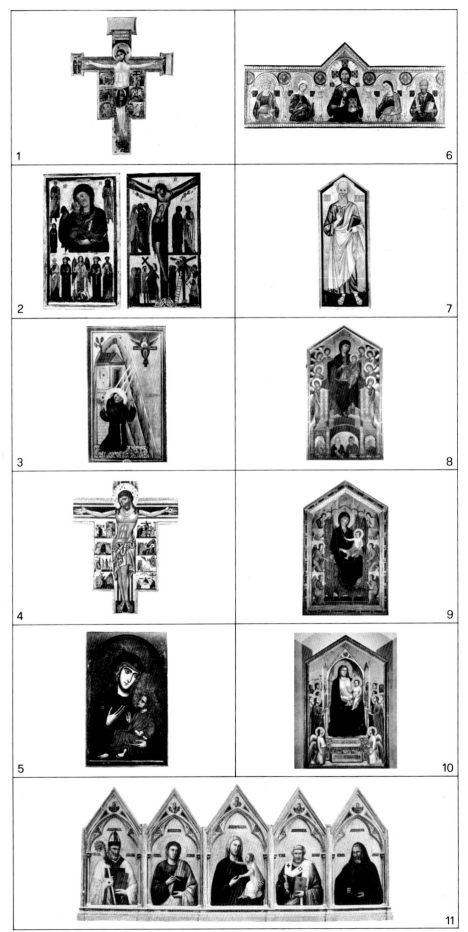

TUSCAN PAINTING OF XII-XIII-XIV CENTURY

TUSCAN SCHOOL (Second Half XII Century)
1. **CRUCIFIX WITH STORIES OF THE PASSION**
   Center: Washing of the Feet, Capture of Christ, Flagellation, Deposition, Lament over the Body Christ, Resurrection.
   Left side: Mourners.
   Right side: Holy Woman.
   (432) Tempera on wood; 2.77 × 2.31.

SCHOOL OF BONAVENTURA BERLINGHIERI (active c. 1228)
2. **DIPTYCH: Left tablet: Madonna and Child with Saints; Right side: Crucifixion with Holy Women, Mourners, Way to Calvary, Deposition.**
   (8574) Tempera on wood; 1.02 × 1.21.
3. **ST. FRANCIS RECEIVING THE STIGMATA**
   (8574) Tempera on wood; 0.80 × 0.51.

SCHOOL OF LUCCA (Middle XIII Century)
4. **CRUCIFIXION WITH STORIES OF THE PASSION**
   Center: Christ before Pilate, Mocking of Christ, Flagellation, Way to Calvary, Crucifixion, Deposition, Holy Women at the Tomb, Supper at Emmaus.
   (434) Tempera on wood; 2.47 × 2.00.

FLORENTINE SCHOOL (Middle XIII Century)
5. **MADONNA AND CHILD (Pisa Madonna)**
   (9213) Tempera on wood; 0,89 × 0,60.

MELIORE DI JACOPO (XIII Century)
6. **ALTARPIECE with Redeemer and SS. Peter, Mary, John the Evangelist and Paul**
   (9153) Tempera on wood; 0.26 × 2.09.
   Signed and dated 1271.
   Tondi with Cherub's heads were added in the XV Century.

MAGDALEN MASTER (Second Half XIII Century)
7. **ST. LUKE THE EVANGELIST**
   (3493) Tempera on wood; 1.20 × 0.38.
   Original painting was discovered in 1935 under two overpaintings of the XIV and the XVIII Centuries.

CIMABUE (c. 1240 - after 1302)
8. **MAESTÀ (Madonna Enthroned) with Angels and Four Prophets**
   (8543) Tempera on wood; 3.85 × 2.23.
   Dateable between 1280-1285.

DUCCIO DI BONINSEGNA (c. 1278 - before 1318)
9. **MAESTÀ (Rucellai Madonna)**
   (unnumbered) Tempera on wood; 4.50 × 2.90.
   Painted in 1285 for the Laudesi order in the Church of Santa Maria Novella.

GIOTTO (1267-1337)
10. **MADONNA IN GLORY with Saints and Angels (Madonna of All Saints)**
    (8344) Tempera on wood; 3.25 × 2.04.
    Dateable around 1310.
11. **MADONNA AND CHILD with SS. Nicholas, John the Evangelist, Peter and Benedict (Polyptych of Badia)**
    (unnumbered) Tempora on wood; 0.91 × 3.40.
    Dateable in the first years of XIV Century.

SIENESE PAINTING OF XIV CENTURY

SIMONE MARTINI (d. 1344)

1. **ANNUNCIATION with SS. Margaret and Asano**
   Spires: Four medallions with prophets Jeremiah, Ezechiel, Isaiah and Daniel. Saints are painted by Lippo Memmi from a design of Simone Martini.
   (451-453) Tempera on wood; 2.65 × 3.05. Signed and dated 1333.

AMBROGIO LORENZETTI (d. 1348)

2. **TWO STORIES OF ST. NICHOLAS**
   (8348) Tempera on wood; 0.96 × 0.53.
3. **TWO STORIES OF ST. NICHOLAS**
   (8349) Tempera on wood; 0,95 × 0.51.
4. **PRESENTATION AT THE TEMPLE**
   Top of center arch: Two prophets.
   (8346) Tempera on wood; 2.57 × 1.68. Signed and dated 1342.

PIETRO LORENZETTI (c. 1280-1348)

5. **MADONNA AND CHILD WITH SS. NICHOLAS AND PROCOLUS**
   Spire: SS. John the Baptist and John the Evangelist.
   (6411) Tempera ond wood; 1,67 × 0.56. (center); 1.45 × 0.93 (sides).
6. **MADONNA AND CHILD IN GLORY with Angels**
   (455) Tempera on wood; 1.45 × 1.22. Signed and dated 1340.
7. **STORIES OF THE LIFE OF THE BLESSED UMILITÀ**
   Polyptych (divided).
   (8347) Tempera on wood; Entire work, including figure of Saint: 1.26 × 0.57; Each panel: 0.44 × 0.32.
   Date 1341 on copy in the storage room. Seven tondi with SS. Jerome, Paul, John the Evangelist, Peter, Antonio, the Virgin and Pietà, from the original painting but displayed in a modern predella.
8. **THREE SPIRES WITH SS. JOHN THE EVANGELIST, MARK AND LUKE**
   (6129) Tempera on wood; 0.51 × 0.21 each. Belonging to number 7.

NICCOLÒ DI SER SOZZO TEGLIACCI (c. 1334-1364)

9. **MADONNA AND CHILD**
   (8349) Tempera on wood; 0.85 × 0.55.

NICCOLÒ BONACCORSI (d. 1388)

10. **PRESENTATION OF THE VIRGIN AT THE TEMPLE**
    (3157) Tempera on wood; 0.50 × 0.34.

SIMONE DEI CROCIFISSI (c. 1330-1399)

11. **NATIVITY**
    (3475) Tempera on wood; 0.46 × 0.25. Bolognese painter of the fourteenth century.

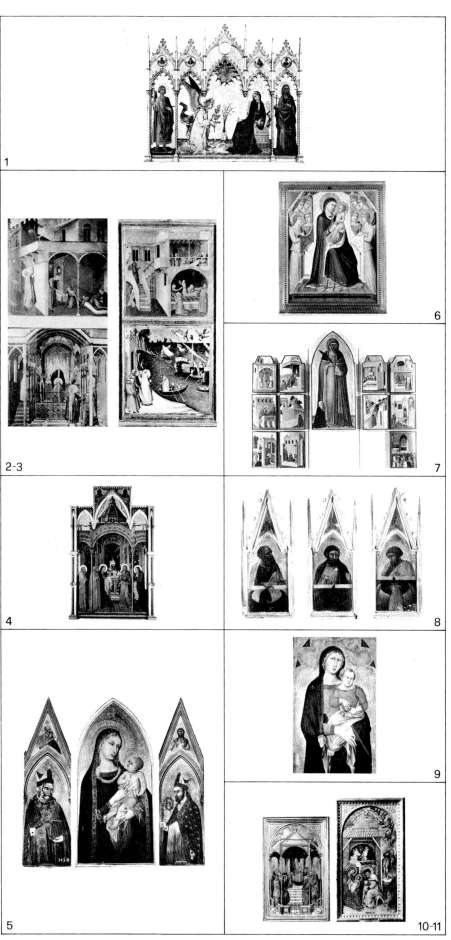

1

2-3

4

5

6

7

8

9

10-11

Duccio: Maestà

Cimabue: Maestà

In the first room of the Uffizi Gallery it is possible to compare directly three superb large paintings on the same theme — the "Maestà", or Madonna and Child Enthroned — and thus to obtain a clear view of Italian painting at one of its earliest turning points.

In Cimabue's *Maestà* (c. 1280, originally on the high altar of the church of Santa Trinita in Florence), the medieval Byzantine tradition is still uppermost, although there are signs of change. In the lower part, four prophets are placed in a restricted, crypt-like space in the arches of the base of the throne, while above them the elaborate throne with the Virgin and Child flanked by angels rises as if into a tall nave. Attempts at perspective have begun to create a sense of depth, although the whole is still dominated by a verticality of composition and a choral effect. The shining, subtly applied gold in the Virgin's cloak is Byzantine, but it helps here to soften the figure; and there is a warmly human note in the way she is pointing to her Child.

In the *Maestà* of the Sienese Duccio (1285, from the Rucellai chapel in the Church of Santa Maria Novella, Florence) the pattern is similar, but treated with a poetic delicacy which will invariably be found in the school of Siena. The throne is less solid than Cimabue's, and the kneeling angels are poised in the golden heaven of the background. The Virgin's cloak has a flowing gilt outline, and the portrayal of the Child is softer and more free.

And lastly, in Giotto's *Maestà* (c. 1310, painted for the church of Ognissanti, Florence) there has been a definite conciliation of a mystical vision with a more human dimension. It is revealed in the more realistic depiction of the throne in space, the solid corporeality of the figures, created by means of chiaroscuro, the controlled but intense emotional relationships.

24

Giotto: Maestà

GOTHIC PAINTING OF XIV-XV CENTURY

AGNOLO GADDI (active 1359-1396)
1. **CRUCIFIXION**
(464) Tempera on wood; 0.575 × 0.77.

LORENZO MONACO (c. 1370-1425)
2. **CORONATION OF THE VIRGIN**
Spires: God the Father, Virgin and Angel
of the Annunciation.
Side panels of frame: Patriarchs and prophets.
Predella panels: Six stories of St. Benedict
and Nativity.
(855) Tempera on wood; Central panel:
3.37 × 4.47; Spires: 1.565 × 0.60.
Signed and dated 1413.
3. **ADORATION OF THE MAGI**
Spire: God the Father and two prophets.
(466) Tempera on wood; 1.44 × 1.77.
Annunciation and two prophets at top
of frame are by an unknown Florentine
painter of the second half of the XV century.

NORTH ITALIAN PAINTER (First Half
XV Century)
4. **ST. BENEDICT EXORCIZING A MONK**
(unnumbered) Tempera on wood; 1.09 × 0.62.
5. **ST. BENEDICT BLESSING
THE POISONED WINE**
(unnumbered) Tempera on wood; 1.11 × 0.66.
6. **ST. BENEDICT PREFORMING
A MIRACLE**
(unnumbered) Tempera on wood; 1.08 × 0.62.

GHERARDO STARNINA (c. 1354-1413)
7. **THEBAID**
(477) Tempera on wood; 0.75 × 2.08.

GENTILE DA FABRIANO
(1360? - c. 1427)
8. **ADORATION OF THE MAGI**
Spires: Cherubim, Angel of the Annunciation
(tondo), two prophets; Cherubim, Christ
Blessing (tondo), Moses and David;
Cherubim, Virgin of the Annunciation (tondo),
two prophets.
Predella panels: Nativity, Flight into Egypt,
Presentation at the Temple (last is a copy;
original in the Louvre).
(8364) Tempera on wood; 3.00 × 2.82.
Signed and dated 1423.
9. **FOUR SAINTS OF THE QUARATESI
POLYPTYCH (SS. Mary Magdalen, John
the Baptist, Nicholas and George**
Spires: Tondi with Angel of the Annunciation,
St. Francis, St. Domenic, Virgin of
the Annunciation, Angels and Cherubim.
(887) Tempera on wood; 1.94 × 0.57 (each).

GIOVANNI DI PAOLO (d. 1482)
10. **MADONNA AND CHILD with SS. Domenic,
Peter, Paul and Thomas Acquinas**
(3255) Tempera on wood; 2.12 × 2.47.
Signed and dated 1445.

JACOPO BELLINI (active 1424-1464)
11. **MADONNA AND CHILD**
(3344) Tempera on wood; 0.73 × 0.57.

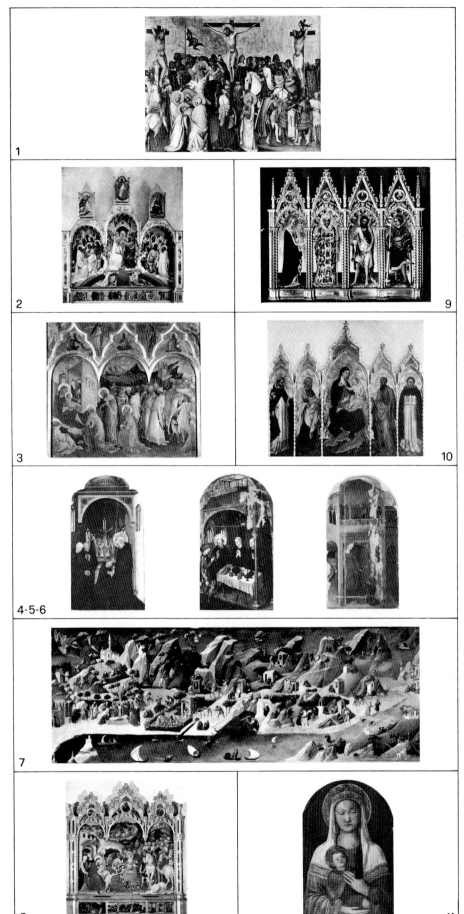

1

2

9

3

10

4-5-6

7

8

11

Ambrogio Lorenzetti: Story of St. Nicholas

The Sienese painters of the four-teenth century — among them the brothers Pietro and Ambrogio Lorenzetti — became acquainted with the innovations of Giotto and used them to express a sensitivity quite different from the strict regard for the essential which characterized the school of Florence.

In this *Story of St. Nicholas*, which originally belonged to a triptych painted for the church of San Procolo during Ambrogio's second stay in Florence (c. 1332-34), the intense blue of the water creates an unmis-takable sense of a vast, deep sea stretching away to the horizon, though beyond it is the usual gold ground of the "primitives". The fleet is depicted with careful realism, and the group of people on the land in the foreground is given variety in the bright colors of their clothes. On the left side is a stretch of crenellated city wall with a gate, above which are greenish rocks, streaked with light, around a little bay.

The lively representation of action (for example the oarsmen) and the sensitivity to nature seem to anticipate the fifteenth—century Renaissance, but these are combined with strokes of fantasy, as in the jutting rocks, balanced by the sails on the horizon. While in the tradition of Giotto the human figure, in its formal aspects, is dominant, people in Ambrogio Lorenzetti's paintings are subordinate to their surroundings and to the rich pictorial mèans used to create them. A century later, in fact, the greatness of Ambrogio was still acknowledged even in Florence: Ghiberti mentions him as a "most famous and unique master".

Simone Martini: Annunciation

Ghiberti preferred Ambrogio Lorenzetti even to Simone Martini, whom the Sienese considered their greatest artist, but he recognized that Simone's paintings were "made with the greatest care and very delicately finished". Simone's *Annunciation* now in the Uffizi (signed and dated 1333) comes from a chapel in the Cathedral of Siena, right from the heart of Florence's rival city. And this extraordinary masterpiece can stand as the symbol of the exquisite "poetry" of Siena as compared to the solid "prose" of Florence.

The line in this work has all the elegance and all the idealistic impetus typical of Gothic painting. In the contours of the two long-limbed and aristocratic figures a continuous tension can be traced from the fluttering robe of the angel to the curved, reluctant posture of the Virgin on her seat. The vase with the splendid lilies, in the center, serves as a connecting link between the two figures. Volume here is subordinate to line; the gilding imbues the objects and figures with the same precious substance the background is made of. Without being restricted by it, the figuration follows the triple rhythm suggested by the frame.

Simone Martini was a friend of Petrarch (as Giotto was of Dante), and had in common with the great poet a capacity for the utmost harmony and evocativeness of idiom. At Avignon, where he spent the last years of his life, he played a decisive part in the formation of the refined "International Gothic" style, which for a considerable period was to dominate the cultural centers of Europe.

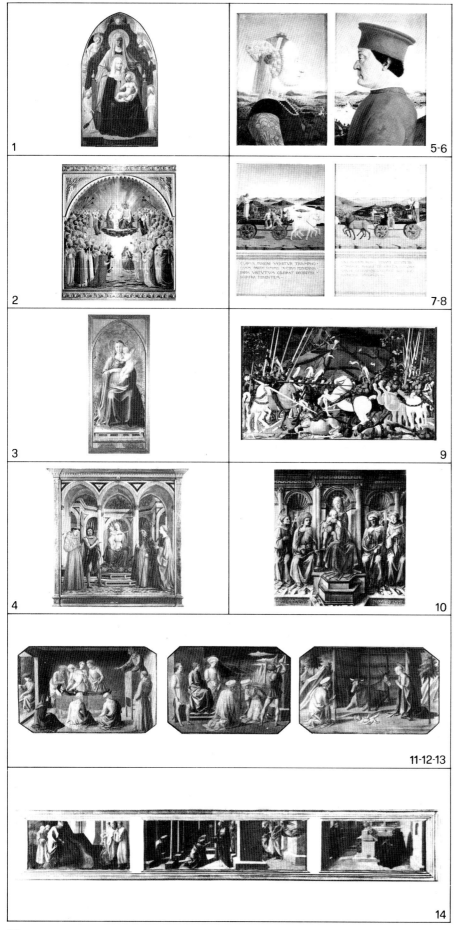

EARLY RENAISSANCE PAINTING

MASACCIO (1401-1428) and **MASOLINO** (1383-1447)
1. **MADONNA AND CHILD WITH ST. ANNE and Five Angels**
   (8386) Tempera on wood; 1.75 × 1.03.

BEATO ANGELICO (c. 1386-1455)
2. **CORONATION OF THE VIRGIN with Saints and Angels**
   (1612) Tempera on wood; 1.14 × 1.13.
3. **MADONNA AND CHILD**
   (143 dep.) Tempera on wood; 1.32 × 0.57.

DOMENICO VENEZIANO (1386-1461)
4. **MADONNA AND CHILD with SS. Francis, John the Baptist, Nicholas and Lucy (Pala dei Magnoli)**
   (884) Tempera on wood; 2.09 × 2.13. Signed.

PIERO DELLA FRANCESCA (1416-1492)
5. **PORTRAIT OF BATTISTA SFORZA**
6. **PORTRAIT OF FEDERIGO DI MONTEFELTRO, DUKE OF URBINO**
7. **ALLEGORICAL TRIUMPH OF FEDERIGO DI MONTEFELTRO**
   Back of number 6.
8. **ALLEGORICAL TRIUMPH OF BATTISTA SFORZA**
   Back of number 5.
   (1615) Tempera on wood; Each panel: 0.47 × 0.33.

PAOLO UCCELLO (1397-1475)
9. **BATTLE OF SAN ROMANO**
   (479) Tempera on wood; 1.82 × 3.23.

FILIPPO LIPPI (c. 1406-1469)
10. **MADONNA AND CHILD ENTHRONED with SS. Francis, Cosmas, Damian, Anthony of Padua**
    (8354) Tempera on wood; 1.96 × 1.96.

FRANCESCO PESELINO (1422-1457)
11. **PREDELLA PANEL: MIRACLE OF ST. ANTHONY**
    (8355) Tempera on wood; 0.32 × 1.44.
12. **PREDELLA PANEL: MARTYRDOM OF SS. COSMAS AND DAMIAN**
    (8355) Tempera on wood; 0.32 × 1.44.
13. **PREDELLA PANEL: NATIVITY**
    (8355) Tempera on wood; 0.32 × 1.44.
    Numbers 11,12 and 13 are part of the Predella of the Madonna of Filippo Lippi (8354); Remaining two stories are in the Louvre (copies are substituted here).

FILIPPO LIPPI (c. 1406-1469)
14. **PREDELLA: St. Frediano Performs a Miracle, Annunciation of the Death of the Virgin, St. Augustine in his Study**
    (8351) Tempera on wood; 0.40 × 2.35. Predella of the Altarpiece of the Barbadori Chapel in Santo Spirito, now in the Louvre.

EARLY RENAISSANCE PAINTING

FILIPPO LIPPI (c. 1406-1469)
1. **CORONATION OF THE VIRGIN**
   with Saints and Angels
   Lower right: The donor; Two tondi on either
   side of central arch: Angel of the
   Annunciation, Virgin of the Annunciation.
   (8352) Tempera on wood; 2.00 × 2.87.
2. **VIRGIN OF THE ANNUNCIATION,**
   ANGEL OF THE ANNUNCIATION,
   ST. ANTHONY ABBOT AND ST. JOHN
   THE BAPTIST
   (8356-8357) Tempera on wood; 1.15 × 0.24
   (each).
3. **ADORATION OF THE CHILD with**
   SS. Hilary, Jerome, Mary Magdalen
   and Angels
   (8350) Tempera on wood; 1.37 × 1.34.
4. **ADORATION OF THE CHILD with Young**
   St. John and St. Romuald
   (8353) Tempera on wood; 1.40 × 1.30.
5. **MADONNA AND CHILD WITH**
   TWO ANGELS
   (1598) Tempera on wood; 0.92 × 0.63.

ALESSO BALDOVINETTI (1425-1499)
6. **MADONNA AND CHILD with SS. Cosmas**
   and Damian, John the Baptist, Laurence,
   Julian and Anthony; kneeling, SS. Francis
   and Domenic
   (487) Tempera on wood; 1.74 × 1.66.
7. **ANNUNCIATION**
   (483) Tempera on wood; 1.67 × 1.37.

LORENZO DI PIETRO CALLED
IL VECCHIETTA (1410-1480)
8. **MADONNA AND CHILD ENTHRONED**
   with SS. Bartholomew, James, Andrew,
   Laurence; kneeling SS. Eligius and Domenic
   (474) Tempera on wood; 1.56 × 2.30.
   Signed and dated 1457.

MATTEO DI GIOVANNI (d. 1495)
9. **MADONNA AND CHILD with St. John**
   the Baptist, Unknown Saint and Two Angels
   (3949) Tempera on wood; 0.64 × 0.48.

BENOZZO GOZZOLI (1420-1497)
10. **PREDELLA PANEL: MYSTIC MARRIAGE**
    OF ST. CATHERINE
    (886) Tempera on wood; 0.25 × 2.24.
11. **PREDELLA PANEL: PIETÀ with SS. John**
    the Evangelist and Mary Magdalen
    (886) Tempera on wood; 0.25 × 2.24.
12. **PREDELLA PANEL: TWO SAINTS**
    (886) Tempera on wood; 0.25 × 2.24.

NEROCCIO DI BARTOLOMEO LANDI
(1447-1500) with **FRANCESCO DI**
GIORGIO MARTINI
13. **PREDELLA: THREE STORIES**
    OF ST. BENEDICT
    (1602) Tempera on wood; 0.28 × 1.93.

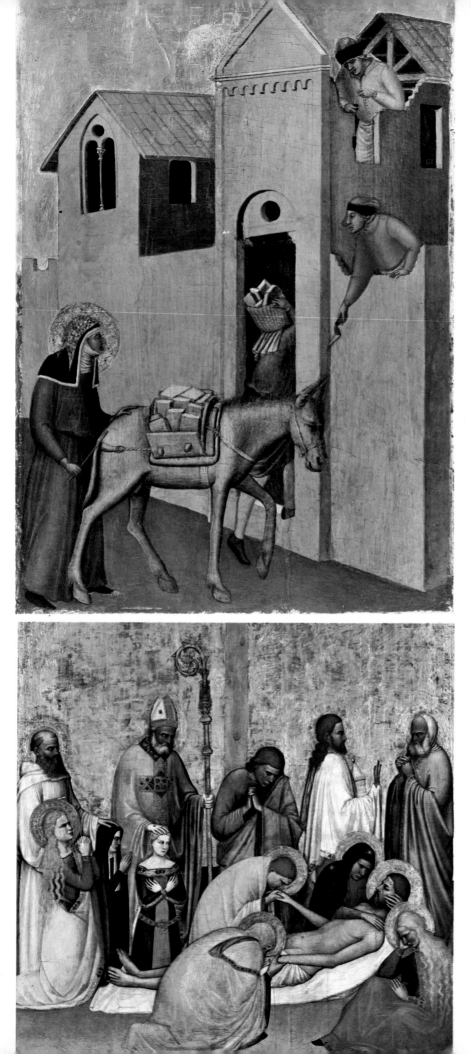

The Uffizi Gallery possesses a rich and representative selection of the works of the greatest Sienese painters of the fourteenth century, among them the *Polyptych of the Blessed Umiltà* by Pietro Lorenzetti (1341), of which one of the side panels with events from the life of Umiltà is reproduced. Generally more dramatic than his brother Ambrogio, Pietro also learnt from Giotto to give solidity to his forms. Here the extreme clarity of the drawing adds pungency to the narrative. The rich coloring is typically Sienese.

Florence itself, although dominated by Giotto and the various artists belonging to his school (Taddeo Gaddi, Bernardo Daddi, the Master of Figline, Maso, Stefano), gradually came to feel the influence of Sienese painting. In the *Pietà* of Giottino (from the church of S. Remigio, and painted late in the century) we can note the passage from the powerfully concise style of Giotto to a looser composition and a more contemplative spirit. The figures are intensely involved in the sorrow of the Deposition, but without losing their composure or crowding too closely around the dead Christ, while the warm and intense coloring, together with the shading of the figures, creates an effect more elegiac than dramatic. The two female figures smaller than the rest (the donors of the work), one of whom is a lady in contemporary costume, carry a hint of the realistic manner of Lombardy, which had been brought to Florence by Giovanni da Milano but which Giottino could have encountered through his father Stefano, who had emigrated to Lombardy, (though the work of the latter has still not been identified). Some scholars believe that this *Pietà* was painted by Maso, Giotto's best pupil, who — perhaps with the mysterious Stefano — came under the influence of Ambrogio Lorenzetti.

The fourteenth century in Florence came to a close with Lorenzo Monaco, of Sienese origin. His large and colorful altarpiece of the *Coronation of the Virgin* (from the church of Santa Maria degli Angeli, where he was in the monastery, signed and dated 1413) shows how persistent archaic modes still were, though the Renaissance was about to dawn. The polyptych is complete with pinnacles, pilasters and predella, and is full of a mystical visionary excitement. The Sienese sharpness of line (as in Simone Martini) is combined with a lively and abstract use of color. The work has thus the fairytale atmosphere typical — in both sacred and profane works — of so-called cosmopolitan Gothis, the last international style, which was to give way to the naturalism of the new century.

Lorenzo Monaco: Coronation of the Virgin

◄
Pietro Lorenzetti: Story of the Blessed Umiltà

◄
Giottino: Pietà

33

Gentile da Fabriano: Adoration of the Magi

In the *Adoration of the Magi* by Gentile da Fabriano, painted in 1423 while the young Masaccio was already at work, International Gothic as it came to an end produced one of its richest and most splendid creations. The altarpiece was painted for the chapel (in the church of Santa Trinita) of the cultured and wealthy Palla Strozzi, and the patron's taste is reflected in the work, with its rich and crowded composition, its lavish use of gold, its exotic details. There are flowers painted on the pilasters and a predella formed of little country and city scenes. This painting reveals Gentile's exceptional talents in the fusion of stylistic elements from diverse sources — from the new Tuscan naturalism to the International Gothic of Lombardy and Siena — but lacks the fundamental decisiveness which was to characterize the new Renaissance. A century later Michelangelo used to say that Gentile ("gentle") had a hand which matched his name.

34

An artist for whom there are historical records but whose identity has not yet clearly emerged is Starnina, supposed to have been the painter of the fascinating *Thebaid* (c. 1410?), though some critics have attributed it to Paolo Uccello or to Angelico in his youth. The picture was in fact not acquired by the Uffizi Gallery until the late eighteenth century, but it could have come from a chapel in the church of the Carmine, where Starnina and Paolo Uccello worked. Or it could be the *Thebaid* by Angelico which is recorded in the Medici Palace. It represents the life of hermits, in many amusing episodes. While it still uses the concise idiom and has the fairy-tale atmosphere of Gothic narrative paintings (and was thus attributed by Lanzi to Pietro Lorenzetti and by Berenson to Maso), there is also to be seen in it a more robust delight in the real world.

With the *Madonna and Child with St. Anne* by Masolino and Masaccio (c. 1424) we find ourselves balanced on the threshold between two epochs. Masolino, although he worked constantly with Masaccio, was still wavering between the traditional and the new. All the soft, doll-like angels here are his, but not the much more energetic one in green at the top right, holding up the drape, which is by Masaccio. Masolino painted also the figure of St. Anne, which is lacking in any real depth of modeling, in spite of the foreshortened hand raised to the head of Jesus in an effort to create space. The dignified, solid, and prominent mass of the Madonna and Child is by Masaccio. Here we find the new "tactile values", brought out by illusionistic modeling which gives to form a sculptural quality through the use of a clear and natural light and contrasting shadows. The picture is simple and strong in its truth to life. The lines of the drapery are not abstract but follow those of the body, the Child is naked and healthy, and there is great energy in the hands of the Virgin clutching her Baby's legs. There is besides a deep moral seriousness in the figures; the Mother is severe and thoughtful, the Child grave, his hand raised in blessing. All these characteristics reveal a new conception of painting, connected with the Humanist sense of the dignity and responsibility of man's destiny on earth. Masaccio was described by his contemporaries as "an excellent imitator of nature, outstanding, universal, a fine composer and without ornamentation", and it is hard to find a better definition of his qualities. In his short life (1401-28) he fulfilled in his art all the aspirations of the early Renaissance, and determined the course of painting for an epoch.

Masolino and Masaccio: Madonna and Child with St. Anne

Starnina: Thebaid, detail

One of the basic elements of the new painting of the fifteenth century was perspective, in the sense of a precise geometrical structure in which forms are dependent on their situation in space. It was Brunelleschi, the genius who completely renewed the science of architecture, who taught perspective to Masaccio, perhaps even collaborating directly in Masaccio's fresco of the *Trinity* in the church of Santa Maria Novella, with its complex and accurate space construction.

Perspective has many and complex laws, not only geometrical but also concerning form, such as "aerial perspective" for distant views dimmed by the atmosphere, relationship between the proportions of the figures and those of the architectural or open-air backgrounds, diminishing clarity of outline as distance increases, and foreshortening of objects to represent their extension in depth. It also requires geometrical analysis and synthesis of bodies.

Though it was applied in the northern Renaissance also, perspective as a decisive element of pictorial structure was understood above all by the Italians, from Masaccio to the mystical Fra Angelico, from Paolo Uccello to Andrea del Castagno and Domenico Veneziano, from Piero della Francesca to Mantegna, Melozzo and the Venetians, from Antonello da Messina to Perugino and Signorelli. In these artists perspective, with its strict laws of construction, became a means for realizing the aspirations of an ideal architecture, based on the concepts of the new Humanism, one of which was the unity of science and art.

One Florentine artist in particular became a fanatic of the new discipline. This was Paolo Uccello, whose almost maniacal dedication to the rendering of perspective is recorded not only in biographical references but above all in his paintings, and in drawings of incredibly concentrated effort. Vasari recounts that Uccello's wife "used to say that all night Paolo stayed in his study to seek for the laws of perspective, and when she called him to sleep he would say: Oh what a sweet thing this perspective is!" For the rest he was of rather anti-naturalistic disposition, inclined to abstraction, and even more bound by the fantasies of the Gothic tradition, for which he was criticized by his contemporaries. But in his magical use of perspective he found the means to create works of powerful effect and such extremely modern taste that they have been called anticipations of Cubism or of metaphysical painting.

Paolo Uccello: Battle of San Romano

The *Battle of San Romano* represents a historical event, a battle of 1432 against the Sienese and troops of the Visconti of Milan which was won by Florence. Paolo Uccello depicted the event in three episodes (one now in the Uffizi, one in the Louvre, and the other in the National Gallery of London), working probably from 1456-57 when the Medici ordered festivities for the *condottiero*

36

Niccolò da Tolentino, who had been in command of the Florentine army.

The three paintings are mentioned in a fifteenth-century inventory of the Medici Palace in via Larga, hanging high up in the bedroom of Piero de' Medici (later that of his son Lorenzo the Magnificent). In 1598, it no longer being remembered what they represented, they were referred to simply as "Ancient Tournaments".

They then appeared in the Wardrobe of the Grand Duchy, where they still were in 1784; but in the following century, probably because their worth was no longer recognized, they were sold, and two of them left Italy.

They constitute, however, probably the most mature masterpiece of Paolo Uccello. The battle scene is constructed in abstract but highly evocative terms, with a brilliant use of per-

spective. Lines lead into the depth of the picture from the broken lances lying in the foreground, the horses and the fallen riders are boldly foreshortened, and forms are reduced to pure volume (the knights in full armor, the palissades of lances, the helmets, bows etc.). In the background are hills, also treated geometrically, but alive with figures of fleeing soldiers and animals.

Fra Angelico: Coronation of the Virgin

The heritage left by Masaccio was taken up and developed during the fifteenth century in Florence in a variety of directions, depending on the individual personalities of the leading artists, and on the general cultural trends of the moment.

One of Masaccio's first "pupils" was undoubtedly Fra Angelico, even if his profound religious conviction, his intense dedication to painting as a sort of visual preaching, and his unwavering continuation of the fourteenth-century mystical tradition made of him, as has been said, a Modernist rather than a truly modern artist. Without the example of Masaccio his radiant figures would not have had also their solidity, nor his settings their concrete reality. Nor would his light have had its day-like quality or his compositions their sure spatial structure.

In his *Coronation of the Virgin* (c. 1435, from Santa Maria Nuova) we can see how even against the celestial gold of the background the arrangement of the figures creates a sense of great depth. And with what clarity and richness of color the saints and angels are characterized in their devout typology!

Fra Filippo Lippi was of quite a different temperament, both as a monk and as a man, as is well known from the story of his life. He also was among the first to be affected by the revolutionary innovations of Masaccio, but he never renounced his instinctive sensuality or the fluid sense of form resulting from it. He was thus influenced also by the reliefs of Donatello, with their fine, dynamic modeling. This famous *Madonna and Child with Angels* (from the Medici villa of Poggio Imperiale) is considered a late work, from about 1465, and we can see how it became a starting point for the young Botticelli. The grace of the group in the foreground, with the Virgin and Child and the two little angels, is complemented by the spring-like atmosphere of the spacious background.

By the time we reach Antonio del Pollaiolo, in the second half of the century, artists are no longer concentrating on the firm and static constructions of the earlier years, but depict a more dynamic, even restless, reality. Pollaiolo uses a flowing line to give a sense of movement to his strongly modeled forms (he was also a great sculptor), and intense, enamel-like colors. This profile *Portrait of a Lady* was formerly attributed to Antonio's less talented brother Piero, but since restoration is considered to be by Antonio himself, as is justified by the elegant but strong portrayal of the aristocratic subject, standing out with warm colors and incisive, mobile line against the sky-blue background.

Filippo Lippi:
Madonna and Child
with Angels

Antonio del Pollaiolo:
Portrait of a Lady

39

Domenico Veneziano: Altarpiece of Santa Lucia dei Magnoli

With Domenico Veneziano we go back to the first half of the fifteenth century, though the elegance of his style and the precision of his analysis mark the turning point between the earlier period and the developments that followed. The minute exactness and richness of his technique can be traced in part to Flemish influence. The altarpiece in the Uffizi comes from the church of Santa Lucia de' Magnoli in Florence, and shows St. Lucy on the right, with Sts. Francis, John the Baptist, and Zenobius; it is signed, and can be dated around 1445. The panels of the predella are now scattered among other collections.

Within an architectural setting (an arcade and a wall with niches) based on accurate and complex perspective study, the scene is composed with perfect symmetry. The gentle natural light enhances the fine drawing and color, and helps to give to the scene an atmosphere of lyrical contemplation, quite different from Masaccio's intense involvement in his subjects.

Domenico Veneziano was the master of Piero della Francesca, the great artist who carried the lessons of the Renaissance beyond the limits of the city of Florence, where he worked only in his early youth, to many other regions of Italy. Piero also absorbed deeply the influence of Flemish painters. In the two magnificent portraits

(c. 1465?) of the Duke and Duchess of Urbino, *Federico da Montefeltro* and *Battista Sforza* — on the back of which are the allegorical *Triumphs* of the two — the breadth of his vision is fully revealed. His "synthesis of form and color in perspective" is one of the highest achievements of the early Renaissance. Federico stands out like a tower, in the geometrical solidity of his profile and the noble impassiveness of his expression, against the spacious background of his domain; the landscape is finely shaded and varied with its lakes, plain, and hills. The human face has an architectural dignity, but the space beyond it gives us a sense of cosmic largeness.

Piero della Francesca: Battista Sforza Piero della Francesca: Federico da Montefeltro

Piero della Francesca: Triumph of Federico da Montefeltro Piero della Francesca: Triumph of Battista Sforza

POLLAIOLO AND BOTTICELLI

ANTONIO (1429-1498) and **PIERO** (1443-1496) **DEL POLLAIOLO**
1. **SS. VINCENT, JAMES AND EUSTACHE** (Altarpiece of the Three Saints). (1617) Tempera on wood; 1.78 × 1.73.
2. **PORTRAIT OF GALEAZZO MARIA SFORZA** (1492) Tempera on wood; 0.65 × 0.43.

ANTONIO DEL POLLAIOLO (1429-1498)
3. **PORTRAIT OF A YOUNG WOMAN** (1491) Tempera on wood; 0.55 × 0.34.

SANDRO BOTTICELLI (1446-1510)
4. **PORTRAIT OF UNKNOWN MAN** with Medal of Cosimo de' Medici (1488) Tempera on wood; 0.57 × 0.44.

ANTONIO DEL POLLAIOLO (1429-1498)
5. **HERCULES AND ANTEUS** (1478) Tempera on wood; 0.16 × 0.09.
6. **HERCULES AND THE HYDRA** (8268) Tempera on wood; 0.17 × 0.12.

PIERO DEL POLLAIOLO (1443-1496)
7. **TEMPERANCE** (495) Tempera on wood; 1.67 × 0.88c.
8. **PRUDENCE** (496) Tempera on wood; 1.67 × 0.88c.
9. **STRENGTH** (497) Tempeera on wood; 1.67 × 0.88c.
10. **FAITH** (498) Tempera on wood; 1.67 × 0.88c.
11. **HOPE** (499) Tempera on wood; 1.67 × 0.88c.
12. **CHARITY** (1610) Tempera on wood; 1.67 × 0.88c. Back: Preliminary design for same figure by Antonio del Pollaiolo.

BOTTICELLI

SANDRO BOTTICELLI (1446-1510)

1. **STRENGTH**
   (1606) Tempera on wood; 1.67 × 0.87.
   Painted in 1470.
2. **MADONNA AND CHILD (Madonna of the Loggia)**
   (8 dep.) Tempera on wood; 0.72 × 0.50.
3. **MADONNA AND CHILD IN GLORY**
   (504) Tempera on wood; 1.20 × 0.65.
4. **MADONNA AND CHILD (Madonna of the Rosegarden)**
   (1601) Tempera on wood; 1.24 × 0.64.
5. **THE RETURN OF JUDITH**
   (1484) Tempera on wood; 0.31 × 0.24.
6. **DISCOVERY OF THE BODY OF HOLOPHERNES**
   (1487) Tempera on wood; 0.31 × 0.25.
7. **ADORATION OF THE MAGI**
   (882) Tempera on wood; 1.11 × 1.34.
8. **ADORATION OF THE MAGI**
   (4346) Tempera on wood; 1.075 × 1.73.
   Unfinished.
9. **MADONNA AND CHILD ENTHRONED**
   with SS. Mary Magdalen, John the Baptist, Cosmas, Damian, Francis and Catherine
   (8657) Tempera on wood; 1.70 × 1.94.
10. **MADONNA AND CHILD ENTHRONED**
    with Two Angels and SS. Catherine, Augustine, Barnaby, John the Baptist, Ignatius and Michael
    (Altarpiece of St. Barnaby).
    (8361) Tempera on wood; 3.40 × 2.70.
11. **SALOMÈ WITH THE HEAD OF THE BAPTIST**
    (8390) Tempera on wood; 0.21 × 0.40.
    Predella panel of number 10.
12. **REMOVING THE HEART OF ST. IGNATIUS**
    (8391) Tempera on wood; 0.21 × 0.38.
    Predella panel of number 10.
13. **PIETÀ**
    (8392) Tempera on wood; 0.21 × 0.41.
    Predella panel of number 10.
14. **ST. AUGUSTINE AND YOUTH AT THE SEA**
    (8393) Tempera on wood; 0.21 × 0.38.
    Predella panel of number 10.

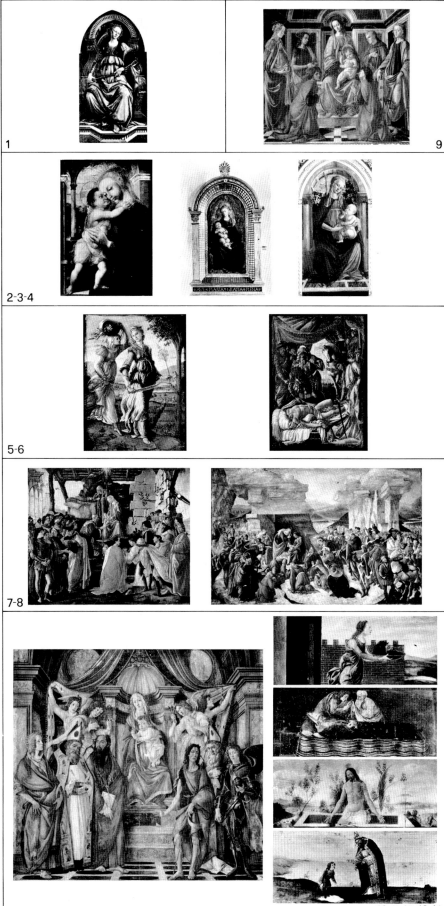

1

9

2-3-4

5-6

7-8

10-11-12-13-14

The height of civilization reached by fifteenth-century Florence under the rule of Lorenzo the Magnificent, the great Medici patron of the arts and of scholars, is fully revealed in the painting of Sandro Botticelli (1444-1510), with its aristocratic spirit and sensitive lyricism. Botticelli's starting point was the mature style of Filippo Lippi, and he was influenced also by the dynamism of Pollaiolo and the fine modeling of Verrocchio. He soon, however, developed a poetic style all his own, in which movement has a sense of musical continuity, the sinuous line refines the forms almost as in Gothic painting (his art has been compared to that of Simone Martini or even of Far Eastern painters), and the decorative effects remove his vision even further from any connection with common reality. Botticelli, as G. C. Argan has recently said, expresses the spirit of contemporary Florentine Neo-Platonic philosophy, the *furor malinconicus* of Marsilio Ficino, "generated by the aspiration to something which one has not, or by nostalgia for something one has lost". Certainly, many changes had occurred in the fifty years since Masaccio expressed his vigorous will in paint. Nonetheless, Botticelli is a strong artist, not at all feminine, as has been suggested. In this respect it is worth quoting an anonymous envoy of Ludovico il Moro of Milan, who reporting to his master in about 1485 on the Florentine artists of the time said of Botticelli that "his things have a virile air".

The *Allegory of Spring* was painted for the Medici villa of Castello, near Florence, for a lesser branch of the family, that of Lorenzo di Pierfrancesco dei Medici. It came to the Uffizi only in 1815. It is the masterpiece of the artist's early maturity, and was probably inspired by Politian's poem *La Giostra*, although the subject has caused much discussion. According to A. Warburg, it is the "reign of Venus", with (right to left) Zephyr, Flora, Flora again as the Hour of Spring, then Venus and the three Graces and Mercury. Another interpretation is that the picture represents the cycle of the seasons.

Against the dark background of the flowery meadow and the orange grove, in an almost watery light, the action is flowing and rhythmical. In the center attention is concentrated on Venus; and the group of the three Graces, whose nakedness is made chaste by veils of incredible delicacy, is musical in its movement. The figures may be inspired by a pagan myth, but they have none of the coldness of a borrowing from archaeology, but rather a nervous vitality which is entirely modern in spirit.

44

Botticelli: Allegory of Spring

9-10-11-12-13

SANDRO BOTTICELLI (1446-1510)
1. **MADONNA AND CHILD with Five Angels**
   (Madonna of the Magnificat)
   (1609) Tempera on wood; tondo:
   diameter 1.15.
2. **MADONNA AND CHILD with Six Angels**
   (Madonna of the Pomegranate)
   (1607) Tempera on wood; tondo:
   diameter 1.43.
3. **PALLAS AND THE CENTAUR**
   (29 dep.) Tempera on wood; 2.07 × 1.48.
4. **BIRTH OF VENUS**
   (878) Tempera on canvas: 1.75 × 2.78.
5. **ALLEGORY OF SPRING (Primavera)**
   (8360) Tempera on wood; 2.03 × 3.14.
6. **ANNUNCIATION**
   (1608) Tempera on wood; 1.50 × 1.56.
7. **ST. AUGUSTINE IN HIS STUDY**
   (1437) Tempera on wood; 0.47 × 0.27.
8. **CALUMNY**
   (1469) Tempera on wood; 0.62 × 0.91.
9. **PREDELLA OF ALTARPIECE OF**
   SAN MARCO: ANNUNCIATION
   (8389) Tempera on wood; 0.21 × 2.69.
10. **PREDELLA OF ALTARPIECE OF**
    SAN MARCO: ST. JEROME REPENTENT
    (8389) Tempera on wood; 0.21 × 2.69.
11. **PREDELLA OF ALTARPIECE OF**
    SAN MARCO: ST. JOHN ON PATMOS
    (8389) Tempera on wood; 0.21 × 2.69.
12. **PREDELLA OF ALTARPIECE OF**
    SAN MARCO: ST. AUGUSTINE IN
    HIS STUDY
    (8389) Tempera on wood; 0.21 × 2.69.
13. **PREDELLA OF ALTARPIECE OF**
    SAN MARCO: MIRACLE OF ST. ELIGIUS
    (8389) Tempera on wood; 0.21 × 2.69.

FLORENTINE PAINTING OF LAST HALF OF XV CENTURY

FILIPPINO LIPPI (c. 1457-1504)
1. **SELF-PORTRAIT**
   (1711) Fresco on tile; 0.50 × 0.31.
2. **ADORATION OF THE CHILD**
   (3246) Tempera on wood; 0.96 × 0.71.
3. **MADONNA AND CHILD with SS. John the Baptist, Victor, Bernard and Zenobius** (Madonna of the Otto).
   (1568) Tempera on wood; 3.55 × 2.55.
   Dated 1486.
   Original frame by Chimenti di Domenico del Tasso.
4. **ST. JEROME**
   (8652) Tempera on wood; 1.36 × 0.71.
5. **ADORATION OF THE MAGI**
   (1566) Tempera on wood; 2.58 × 2.43.
   Signed and dated 1496.
6. **PORTRAIT OF OLD MAN**
   (1485) Fresco on tile; 0.47 × 0.38.
7. **ALLEGORY**
   (8378) Tempera on wood, 0.30 × 0.23.

BARTOLOMEO DI GIOVANNI
(Last Half of XV Century)
8. **MIRACLE OF ST. BENEDICT**
   (1502) Tempera on wood; 0.32 × 0.375.
9. **MIRACLE OF ST. BENEDICT**
   (3154) Tempera on wood; 0.32 × 0.30.

JACOPO DEL SELLAIO (c. 1442-1493)
10. **TRIUMPH OF MORDECAI**
    (493) Tempera on wood; 0.44 × 0.81.
11. **BANQUET OF AHASUERAS**
    (491) Tempera on wood; 0.44 × 0.81.
12. **BANQUET OF QUEEN VASTI**
    (492) Tempera on wood; 0.44 × 0.81.

1

7

2

8

3

9

4

10

5

11

6

12

The collection of Botticelli's works in the Uffizi is exceptional in itself, and one of the high points of a tour of the Gallery.

The *Birth of Venus* forms a pair with *Spring*; it was also painted for the villa of Castello. It is usually dated around 1486, although one critic has placed it much earlier, seeing in it an allusion to the love of Giuliano dei Medici (murdered in the famous Pazzi conspiracy in 1478) for Simonetta Cattaneo Vespucci, who lived at Portovenere (port of Venus) on the Tyrrhenian coast.

Although the subject — Venus, born of the sea, being sped by two Zephyrs towards land, while an Hour hurries to cover her with a cloak — is quite clear, there has been much discussion as to the sources of the imagery and the exact allegorical significance. Some critics interpret it as Beauty (Venus) being born of the union of Spirit with Matter, or Idea with Nature. And we can certainly see as an incarnation of pure beauty the figure in the midst of the wide and luminous seascape, even if her loveliness, for all its freshness, has overtones of subtle melancholy.

Pallas and the Centaur (also from Castello, c. 1485) is for some critics a political allegory, turning on Lorenzo the Magnificent's mission of 1479-80 to Naples (to which the bay in the background would be a reference) — when he persuaded the King to break off his war on Florence — or on his subjugation of the Pazzi conspiracy. In fact the emblem of the diamond rings on the dress of Pallas is Medicean. For others the subject is the reconciliation of wisdom (Minerva) with the instincts (the Centaur).

The composition itself is based on the play of opposites — the balance of horizontal and vertical elements, the contrast of the luminously spiritual Minerva and the darkly animal Centaur, the hard rocks at the side and the soft expanse of water beyond — and lends force to the notion that the painting has a moral basis. Its theme would thus be the construction of harmony out of strife.

The *Madonna of the Magnificat* (c. 1482), on the other hand, is a fine example of Botticelli's religious painting. The figures in this tondo are designed to emphasize the circular form, and the representation has both rich beauty and persuasive tenderness.

Botticelli: Pallas and the Centaur

◀

Botticelli: Birth of Venus, detail

▶

Botticelli: Madonna of the Magnificat

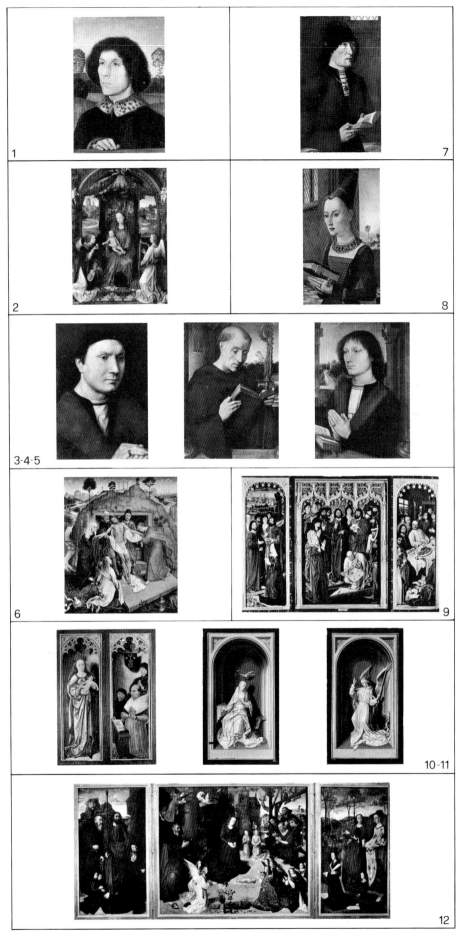

1

7

2

8

3-4-5

6

9

10-11

12

FLEMISH PAINTING OF XV CENTURY

HANS MEMLING (c. 1433-1494)
1. **PORTRAIT OF A MAN IN LANDSCAPE**
   (1102) Oil on wood; 0.38 × 0.27.
2. **MADONNA AND CHILD ENTHRONED WITH TWO ANGELS**
   (1024) Oil on wood; 0.57 × 0.42.
3. **PORTRAIT OF UNKNOWN MAN**
   (1101) Oil on wood; 0.35 × 0.25.
4. **ST. BENEDICT**
   (1090) Oil on wood; 0.45 × 0.34.
5. **PORTRAIT OF BENEDETTO DI TOMMASO PORTINARI**
   (1100) Oil on wood; 0.45 × 0.34.

ROGIER VAN DER WEYDEN
(1400-1464)
6. **DEPOSITION**
   (1114) Oil on wood; 1.10 × 0.96.

MASTER OF THE BARONCELLI PORTRAIT
7. **PORTRAIT OF PIERANTONIO BARONCELLI**
   (8405) Oil on wood; 0.56 × 0.31.
8. **PORTRAIT OF MARIA BONCIANI, WIFE OF PIERANTONIO BARONCELLI**
   (8405) Oil on wood; 0.56 × 0.31.

NICOLAS FROMENT (active 1461-1476)
9. **TRYPTYCH: central panel RESURRECTION OF LAZARUS; left panel: MARTHA AT THE FEET OF CHRIST; right panel: MARY MAGDALEN WASHES THE FEET OF CHRIST**
   (1065) Oil on wood; central panel: 1.75 × 1.34; side panels: 1.75 × 0.66 each.
10. **TRYPTYCH: outside left panel: MADONNA AND CHILD; outside right panel: THE DONORS**
   (1065) Oil on wood; 1.75 × 0.66 each.
   Signed and dated 1461.

HUGO VAN DER GOES (c. 1440-1482)
11. **PORTINARI ALTARPIECE: VIRGIN OF THE ANNUNCIATION** (outside left panel); **ANGEL OF THE ANNUNCIATION** (outside right panel)
12. **PORTINARI ALTARPIECE: ADORATION OF THE SHEPHERDS** (central panel); **TOMMASO PORTINARI AND HIS SONS** with Two Saints (left panel); **MARIA PORTINARI AND HER DAUGHTER** with Two Saints (right panel)
   (3191, 3192, 3193) Oil on wood; central panel: 2.53 × 3.04; side panels: 2.53 × 1.41 (each).

FLORENTINE PAINTING OF THE XV-XVI CENTURY

FRANCESCO BOTTICINI (d. 1498)
1. **TOBIAS AND THE ANGEL**
   (8359) Tempera on wood; 1.53 × 1.54.

ANDREA VERROCCHIO (1435-1488)
2. **BAPTISM OF CHRIST**
   (8358) Oil on wood; 1.77 × 1.51.
   Collaboration.

LEONARDO DA VINCI (1452-1519)
3. **ANNUNCIATION**
   (1618) Oil on wood; 0.98 × 2.17.
4. **ADORATION OF THE MAGI**
   (1594) Undercoat of paint on wood;
   2.43 × 2.46.

DOMENICO GHIRLANDAIO
(1449-1494)
5. **ADORATION OF THE MAGI**
   (1619) Oil on wood; tondo; diameter: 1.71.
6. **MADONNA AND CHILD ENTHRONED
   WITH SAINTS** Dionysius, Aeropagita,
   Domenic, Clement, and Thomas Acquinas
   Predella: Pietà (center); Stories of the
   SS. above.
   (8388-8387) Oil on wood; Altarpiece
   1.68 × 1.97; Predella; 0.18 × 2.27.
7. **MADONNA AND CHILD ENTHRONED
   WITH SAINTS** Michael, Justus, Zenobis
   and Raphael
   (881) Oil on wood; 1.90 × 2.00.

LORENZO DI CREDI (1459-1537)
8. **ADORATION OF THE SHEPHERDS**
   (8399) Oil on wood; 2.24 × 1.96.
9. **ANNUNCIATION**
   Below: Creation of Eve, Original Sin,
   Expulsion from Paradise.
   (1597) Oil on wood; 0.88 × 0.71.
10. **YOUNG MAN WITH RED CAP**
    (1490) Oil on wood; 0.53 × 0.35.
11. **VENUS**
    (3094) Oil on canvas; 1.51 × 0.69.
12. **MADONNA AND CHILD WITH YOUNG
    ST. JOHN AND TWO ANGELS**
    (3244) Oil on wood; tondo; diameter: 0.71.

PIERO DI COSIMO (1462-1521)
13. **IMMACULATE CONCEPTION** with Six SS.
    (506) Oil on wood; 2.06 × 1.72.
14. **MADONNA AND CHILD WITH
    MUSICAL ANGEL**
    (3885) Oil on wood; 1.16 × 0.83.
    Now in Palazzo Davanzati.
15. **SACRIFICE FOR THE LIBERATION
    OF ANDROMEDA**
    (509) Oil on wood; 0.67 × 1.51.
    Attributed.
16. **PERSEUS LIBERATING ANDROMEDA**
    (1536) Oil on wood; 0.71 × 1.23.

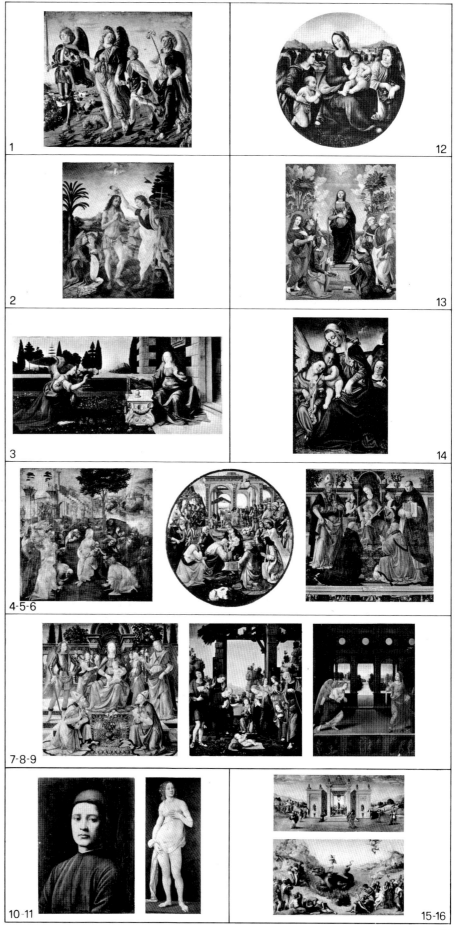

1

12

2

13

3

14

4-5-6

7-8-9

10-11

15-16

Van der Goes: Portinari Triptych

▶

Van der Weyden: Entombment

Florentine artists became acquainted with the contemporary Flemish school of painting probably about 1440, when the lively commercial interchange between the two regions and the presence of Florentine bankers in Flanders ensured continuous contacts. Lorenzo the Magnificent possessed a *St. Jerome* by Jan van Eyck.

But a more direct connection was made when Rogier van der Weyden came to Italy for the Jubilee in Rome in 1450. Two of his works — a *Virgin and Saints* in Frankfurt, painted for the Medici, and the *Entombment of Christ* in the Uffizi — prove that the passed though Florence, because he uses stylistic elements derived from Florentine works (in the *Virgin and Saints* from Domenico Veneziano, and in the *Entombment* from Fra Angelico).

The *Entombment*, however, is not recorded as being in the Medici collections until the seventeenth century. The landscape (not Italian, but Nordic) at the sides of the rocky tomb gives a sense of vastness, while the details, even down to the wrinkles on one of the faces, are analyzed with minute realism. The spirit of the painting as a whole is of a sorrowful but calm intimacy. Michelangelo spoke almost with scorn of this Flemish manner of expressing devotion, as compared with the more intellectual character of the Italians. But the capacity to unify a work through the effect of light is possessed by van der Weyden (a pupil of van Eyck) to a far greater degree than by the Florentines.

If the brief contact with van der Weyden had no evident influence on Florentine artists, the same cannot be said of the great triptych of Hugo van der Goes, the most famous painter of the later fifteenth century in Flanders. The outstanding characteristic of this artist was a certain monumentality which gave him an immediate affinity with the Italians; he had besides a dramatic sense of composition, a capacity to create vast and sensuous landscapes for his backgrounds, and a strong feeling for realism. There is no need to suppose he ever made a journey to Italy, as he could well have felt the influence of the southern Renaissance through works owned by the agents of the Medici banks in Flanders.

It was for one of these, Tommaso Portinari, that he painted in Bruges (about 1476-78) the huge triptych (it was Portinari himself who wanted it so large) now in the Uffizi. It was sent by sea to Florence and placed on the high altar of the church of Santo Egidio, in the Portinari family chapel, where it was surrounded by frescoes by Domenico Veneziano, Piero della Francesca, Andrea del Castagno and Baldovinetti, now unfortunately all lost. The two great schools of paintings could thus be compared side by side.

On the back of the outer panels of the triptych the *Annunciation* is depicted in monochrome. Opened up it represents, in brilliant colors, the *Adoration of the Child Jesus*; in the left panel Sts. Anthony Abbot and Thomas present Tommaso Portinari and his two little sons, and in the right one Sts. Margareth and Mary Magdalen present his wife Maria and their daughter. In the landscape in the background are portrayed other episodes from the nativity.

From the point of view of style, the triptych is strangely empty in the center; the child Jesus lies on the ground irradiating light, and at a distance the adoring figures, of sizes varying according to their importance, form a circle around him. This creates a theatrical effect, which is enhanced by the other elements of the painting: the warm colors, the fervor of the act of adoration, the spacious landscape, the splendid naturalism of details like the flowers and the sheaf of straw in the foreground, the passage from the most delicate touches to others of rude realism, as in the figures of the shepherds.

This work, with its symphonic complexity, made a strong impression on the artists of Florence, as the other paintings in the same room show; Filippino Lippi, Ghirlandaio, Lorenzo di Credi, Botticini, perhaps even Leonardo were all in their own way influenced by it.

Van der Goes: Portinari Triptych, detail

RENAISSANCE PAINTING OF CENTRAL ITALY

GIOVANNI BOCCATI (active 1435-1480)
1. **MADONNA AND CHILD with Four Angels and Seraphim**
(3578) Tempera on wood; 0.64 × 0.47.

BARTOLOMEO CAPORALI
(1420? - 1505?)
2. **MADONNA AND CHILD with Four Angels**
(3250) Tempera on wood; 0.79 × 0.55.

ANTONIAZZO ROMANO (active 1460-1508)
3. **MADONNA AND CHILD**
(2199) Tempera on wood; 0.64 × 0.45.
Dated 1482.
4. **TRYPTYCH WITH MADONNA AND CHILD**
Left panel: St. Peter and Angel of the Annunciation
Right panel: St. Paul and Virgin of the Annunciation
(3274) Tempera on wood; Center: 0.73 × 0.44; Panels: 0.73 × 0.21 each.
Dated 1485.

LUCA SIGNORELLI (1441-1523) and **PIETRO PERUGINO** (1446-1523)
5. **CRUCIFIX with SS. Jerome, Francis, Mary Magdalen, John the Baptist and the Blessed Giovanni Colombini**
(3425) Oil on wood; 2.07 × 1.83.

LUCA SIGNORELLI (1441-1523)
6. **PREDELLA PANEL: ANNUNCIATION**
(1613) Oil on wood; 0.21 × 2.10.
7. **PREDELLA PANEL: ADORATION OF THE SHEPHERDS**
(1613) Oil on wood; 0.21 × 2.10.
8. **PREDELLA PANEL: ADORATION OF THE MAGI**
(1613) Oil on wood; 0.21 × 2.10.
9. **THE TRINITY with Madonna and Child, Archangels Michael and Gabriel and SS. Augustine and Anastasius**
(8369) Oil on wood; 2.78 × 1.88.
10. **HOLY FAMILY**
(1605) Oil on wood; tondo, diameter: 1.24.
11. **MADONNA AND CHILD: Background: Allegorical Figures; Above: Trinity (center), Two Prophets (sides)**
(502) Oil on wood; 1.70 × 1.15.
12. **CRUCIFIX WITH MARY MAGDALEN**
(8368) Oil on canvas; 2.49 × 1.66.
13. **ALLEGORY OF FERTILITY**
(3107) Oil (monochrome and grisaille) on wood; 0.61 × 1.09.
14. **PREDELLA PANEL: LAST SUPPER**
(8271) Oil on wood; 0.32 × 2.10.
15. **PREDELLA PANEL: AGONY IN THE GARDEN**
(8371) Oil on wood; 0.32 × 2.10.
16. **PREDELLA PANEL: FLAGELLATION**
(8371) Oil on wood; 0.32 × 2.10.

RENAISSANCE PAINTING OF CENTRAL ITALY

MELOZZO DA FORLÌ (1438-1494)
1. **ANGEL OF THE ANNUNCIATION**
   (3341) Oil on wood; 1.16 × 0.60.
   On the back: unfinished painting
   of Evangelist.
2. **VIRGIN OF THE ANNUNCIATION**
   On the back: unfinished painting of Bishop.
   (3343) Oil on wood; 1.16 × 0.60.

PIETRO PERUGINO (1446-1523)
3. **MADONNA AND CHILD with SS. John
   the Baptist and Sebastian**
   (1435) Oil on wood; 1.78 × 1.64.
4. **PIETÀ**
   (8365) Oil on wood; 1.68 × 1.76.
5. **PORTRAIT OF FRANCESO DELLE OPERE**
   (1700) Oil on wood; 0.51 × 0.43.
   Signed and dated 1494.
6. **PORTRAIT OF DON BIAGIO MILANESI**
   (8375) Oil on wood; 0.28 × 0.26.
7. **PORTRAIT OF BALASSARRE
   VALLOMBROSANO**
   (8376) Oil on wood; 0.26 × 0.27.
8. **PORTRAIT OF YOUNG MAN**
   (1474) Oil on wood; 0.37 × 0.26.

LORENZO COSTA (1460-1535)
9. **PORTRAIT OF GIOVANNI BENTIVOGLIO**
   (8384) Tempera on wood; 0.55 × 0.49.
   Signed.

FRANCESCO FRANCIA (c. 1450-1517)
10. **PORTRAIT OF EVANGELISTA SCAPPI**
    (1444) Tempera on wood; 0.55 × 0.44.

ALESSANDRO ARALDI (c. 1460-1528)
11. **PORTRAIT OF BARBARA PALLAVICINO**
    (8383) Tempera on wood; 0.50 × 0.46.

GIOVANNI FRANCESCO DE' MAINERI
(active 1489-1504)
12. **CHRIST CARRYING CROSS**
    (3348) Oil on wood; 0.42 × 0.50.

LORENZO COSTA (1460-1535)
13. **ST. SEBASTIAN**
    (3282) Tempera on wood; 0.55 × 0.33.

MARCO PALMEZZANO (1456-1538)
14. **CRUCIFIXION with Mourners, Holy Woman
    and St. Mary Magdalen**
    (1418) Tempera on wood; 1.14 × 0.91.
    Signed.

GIROLAMO GENGA (1476-1551)
15. **MARTYRDOM OF ST. SEBASTIAN**
    (1535) Tempera on wood; 0.98 × 0.83.

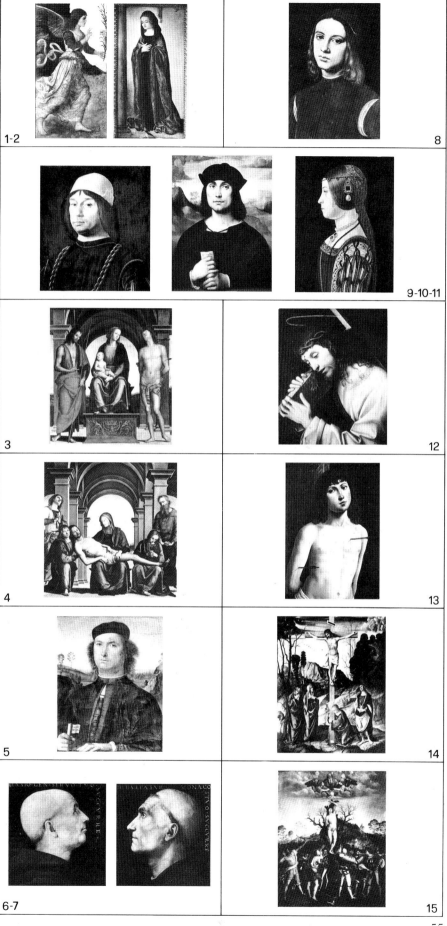

1-2

8

9-10-11

3

12

4

13

5

14

6-7

15

Hans Memling (c. 1433-1494) was one of the first of the Flemish primitives to be appreciated by students of the last century. This fact, together with the number and quality of his known works, has given rise to his fame as a typical representative of the Flemish school of painting. Active in Bruges, he was a craftsman of great technical precision, and his quietly emotional devoutness impresses us with its sincerity.

There are several of his works in the Uffizi, among them a youthful portrait of a *Man in a Landscape* (c. 1470), and this *St. Benedict*. It forms a pair with a *Portrait of Benedetto Portinari*, and the two were originally in a triptych with a Madonna now in Berlin, dated 1487. Memling in fact worked for Florentine residents of Bruges, such as the Portinaris, and Angelo Tani, for whom he painted a large *Last Judgment*. This painting, however, instead of coming to Florence as intended, was captured by pirates and reached the end of its adventures in the Marienkirche of Danzig. Vasari mentions works by Memling in Florence in the possession of the Medici.

Memling:
St. Benedict

Filippino Lippi:
Adoration of the Magi

Ghirlandaio: Adoration of the Magi

Filippino Lippi (d. 1504) is one of the leading Florentine artists of the later fifteenth century, and is representative of the restless style with which the century ended. He was the son of Fra Filippo Lippi, and worked at first in the manner of the young Botticelli — so much so that his youthful works used to be attributed simply to a "friend of Sandro". He then had the good fortune to complete the frescoes left unfinished by Masaccio in the church of the Carmine, a task which he performed worthily. Later, however, while he developed a virtuosity of technique rivaling the Flemings, his style became marked by a fanciful brilliance;

which in the frescoes in Santa Maria sopra Minerva in Rome and those in the Strozzi chapel of Santa Maria Novella in Florence takes on pre-Baroque accents.

The *Adoration of the Magi* in the Uffizi, signed and dated 1496, was painted for the monks of San Donato at Scopeto, who in 1481 had commissioned a painting on the same subject of Leonardo da Vinci. Leonardo's unfinished work (also in the Uffizi) influenced Filippino in the composition in his version; here also a circle of eager figures presses around the Madonna and Child. The people portrayed, however, are quite different in type; Filippino's are bi-

zarre and stylized. His whole scene, even to the landscape with the procession of the Magi, is pervaded by an intense excitement.

Yet another *Adoration of the Magi* is depicted in the tondo by Domenico Ghirlandaio (1487). The scene here has far greater composure, and the style is richly descriptive. The refined classical architecture of the setting reveals the artist's great talent as an illustrator; his fresco cycles in the churches of Santa Trinita and Santa Maria Novella are still one of the most important visual documents of the splendors of everyday life during the Florentine Renaissance.

Verrocchio: Baptism of Christ

Andrea del Verrocchio (1453-1488) was a great sculptor who worked also as a painter; his drawing is energetic and incisive, and his strongly modeled and highly refined forms are enlivened by vibrant chiaroscuro. The problem of collaboration in his works, however, is complicated; among others, Leonardo da Vinci himself was apprenticed to Verrocchio in his youth.

In this *Baptism of Christ*, painted for the church of San Salvi and attributed by historical sources to Verrocchio, critics have noted stylistic incongruities which have been variously interpreted. According to the view now most generally held, the painting was begun in about 1470 by Verrocchio, who did the too harsh figure of St. John, the compact and rocky landscape on the right, and the forward-facing angel with the finely sculptured head. Leonardo, still an adolescent, subsequently made his contribution to the work, painting the much more graceful angel in profile on the left and the receding landscape on the same side, with its fine shading.

The painting, finally, was completed by Verrocchio, with the sculptural but freer figure of Christ, though Leonardo or perhaps Lorenzo di Credi are believed to have had a hand here also. Some critics have thought they saw traces of further collaborators, including Botticelli and Botticini. This work, in any case, while it sums up the characteristics of fifteenth-century Florentine painting — vigorous structure with a sense of the monumental, and expertly precise drawing — heralds at the same time the new, Leonardesque vision of nature, less sharply defined in form, but more penetrating in intellect and feeling.

Melozzo da Forlì (1438-1494), on the other hand, does not belong to the Florentine school, but starts out from the example of Piero della Francesca to develop a style in which perspective creates a solemn structural quality, as can be seen in his fresco of Sixtus IV inaugurating the Library in the Vatican Pinacoteca. He later painted some large foreshortened figures for the church of the Santi Apostoli in Rome (among them the famous musician angels), with a warmth and strength that brought the aristocratic idiom of Piero closer to popular taste. He worked also at Urbino, Loreto, Ancona and Forlì, with considerable influence (for example on Antoniazzo Romano). In the Uffizi there are two fragmentary panels by him, with the lower part of a St. Benedict and a St. John the Baptist, and on the backs the Angel and the Virgin of the *Annunciation*, unfortunately very much retouched.

Melozzo da Forlì: Angel of the Annunciation

The genius of Leonardo da Vinci (1452-1519) was many-sided; he was influential in both architecture and sculpture, and he made many scientific experiments and inventions, often far ahead of his times. His greatness, however, reveals itself most truly in painting, which he himself considered the most excellent of the arts.

In his *Treatise on Painting* he describes art as something superior to mere imitation, and even to the reality of nature; for him art was akin to divinity. "The painter who depicts from pratice and the judgment of his eye, *without reasoning*, is like a mirror, which imitates all the things placed before it without knowledge of them." Reason, or the scientific spirit, therefore, is needed. "The painter is master of all the things which can occur to human thought... And in fact all that is in the universe, in essence, presence or imagination, he has first in his mind and then in his hands..." The painter, then, must be in possession not only of the outward phenomena of nature, but also of its inner structures and potentialities, which become an integral part of his vision. "Simple natural things are finite, and the works which the eye orders the hand to create are infinite." "The divinity belonging to the science of painting transforms the painter's mind into an image of the mind of God, since he has power and freedom to bring to life diverse essences of animals, plants, villages, countrysides, ruins of mountains, fearful and frightening places..."

But on the other hand Leonardo feels the enormous mystery of nature, which never allows the work of art entirely to capture reality. "If any artist should let himself believe that he was able to store up in himself all the forms and effects of nature, certainly he would seem to me to be possessed of great ignorance; because those effects are infinite, and our memory is not of sufficient capacity."

From a practical point of view, his theories led the artist to make many preliminary drawings, some of which are scientifically objective, while others poetically transform external reality. And in his paintings, form no longer stands apart — as it did in the work of the Florentine painters who preceded him — set off by the incisive drawing and sculptural effects of chiaroscuro, but is absorbed into the whole through *sfumato* — that is, a slight darkening of the space about it which softens its outlines or, better, a half light, as "when evening is falling... and it is bad weather", which bestows "grace and sweetness" on the natural world. The individuality of each object is clarified, but at the same time is fused in the whole, and reality is veiled in mystery.

60

Leonardo da Vinci: Annunciation

The *Annunciation* in the Uffizi comes from the monastery of San Bartolomeo at Monteoliveto near Florence, and was traditionally attributed to Domenico Ghirlandaio. Vasari does not mention the work. Brought to the Uffizi in 1867, it was first attributed to Leonardo by Liphart (1869); on mature consideration a long line of connoisseurs, from W. Bode and A. Venturi to B. Berenson, K. Clark and G. Castelfranco concurred with this judgment. There is besides in Oxford a drawing by Leonardo for the right sleeve of the angel, and one in the Louvre for the Madonna's cloak. But even this is not conclusive proof (the drawings could have been made from rather than for the painting), and as many equally authoritative critics disagreed, among them G. Morelli, G. B. Cavalcaselle,

L. H. Heydenreich and G. Calvi. They proposed among others as authors of the work Domenico Ghirlandaio, or Ridolfo del Ghirlandaio, or Verrocchio and Lorenzo di Credi in collaboration.

They also pointed out the "defects" in the painting as compared to other works by the great master: the conventional arrangement of the scene, with the two figures, one on each side, in the foreground; an uncertainty in the placing of the Virgin, the academic over-abundance of her clothes and a certain coldness in her very beautiful face; the too precisely drawn curl on the angel's forehead; and the fact that in the landscape in the background there are boats and a little town, while in other works by Leonardo the nature against which the figures are portrayed is without

any further sign of human presence. X-ray examination has also shown that the angel originally stood with his head more bowed, looking at the ground.

However, in spite of such objections the painting is now almost universally attributed to Leonardo. It would have been made while he was still very young (c. 1472-75), an apprentice among others in the workshop of Verrocchio, and he probably worked on it off and on over a long period, which would explain the lack of momentum that would have given the work more strength. It remains, however, beyond the capacities of a Ghirlandaio or of any other of Verrocchio's pupils.

The scene takes place on a flowery lawn in front of an aristocratic villa of Florentine style, with the Virgin

sitting before a lectern placed on a marble table, richly carved in the manner of Verrocchio. The position of the Virgin is almost frontal, the building forming a background for her, while in counterbalance the angel is represented in profile, his whole figure tense in the attitude of annunciation, with the open landscape behind him. Halfway up the painting is a balustrade separating the quiet scene from the landscape beyond, which after a curtain of trees recedes away to distant lakes and mountains. The gentle spirit of the whole, the exactness of every detail of the foreground, and the cosmic spaciousness and shading of the landscape are already manifestly Leonardesque, although the *sfumato* technique has not yet been applied to the two figures, which have definite outlines.

61

Leonardo da Vinci: Adoration of the Magi

In 1481 Leonardo accepted a commission from the monks of San Donato at Scopeto for an *Adoration of the Magi*, to be ready in not longer than thirty months, but in 1482 he moved to Milan, and left it unfinished in the house of Amerigo Benci. In the seventeenth century it came into the possession of the Medici, and passed later to the Uffizi. The date of this work is hard to believe, so far is it stylistically in advance of its times; and E. Müntz, for example, would not allow that it was earlier

than 1500.

Putting aside previous iconographical tradition with all the details of the procession of the Magi (it is interesting to note that in a preparatory drawing in the Louvre the ass and the ox are still to be seen), Leonardo concentrated the scene in a circle of intensely involved figures around the Virgin and Child, while in the background ruined buildings, and figures engaged in wild combat, refer perhaps to the downfall of the pagan world. The pyramidal composition of the

central group, the intense expressiveness of the human figures, the emotional and intellectual impact of the scene with its enigmatic overtones, the new dramatic monumentality of form, make of this painting of 1481 the first work belonging in essence to the sixteenth century.

Its powerful qualities should be compared, for instance, with the flowing but cold grace, technically excellent, of the *Annunciation* of Lorenzo di Credi (1455-1537), probably this painter's masterpiece.

Lorenzo di Credi: Annunciation

Signorelli: Holy Family

Perugino:
Portrait of Francesco delle Opere

Luca Signorelli (c. 1450-1523) was a pupil of Piero della Francesca, but quite different in temperament. Instead of the contemplative impassivity and mathematical harmony of his master, the style he developed had a proud and dynamic energy, concentrated in the human body, and a robust color sense with particular bronze chiaroscuro tints. He showed his vigorous narrative gifts in the decoration of the cloister of Monteoliveto, and crowned his career with the famous frescoes in the Cathedral of Orvieto, depicting the end of the world.

The tondo in the Uffizi with the *Holy Family* was painted for the council hall of the Captains of the Guelph Party, and is probably close in date to the Orvieto frescoes. The strong figures of Mary and Joseph fit the curve of the tondo while the centrally placed Child is on the same vertical line as the two open books. The sense of monumental unity, severe and highly sculptural, anticipates Michelangelo.

The chief representative of Umbrian painting in the Uffizi is Pietro Vannucci, called Perugino (1445-1524), who also started out from the sphere of Piero della Francesca. From Piero he learned how to create perspective, while he looked to Verrocchio for refinement of form and harmony of line. Both these influences are present in Perugino's part of the *Stories of St. Bernardino* in the Gallery of Perugia. In the *Christ Giving the Keys to St. Peter* (1481-82), the fresco which he contributed to the decoration of the Sistine Chapel we find the same combination. The background is a vast square, given rhythm by the pattern of the marble paving and symmetry by the temple in the middle and the triumphal arches at the sides; while the figures themselves, divided into two matching groups, are full of life.

Perugino's balanced style was particularly suitable for the representation of religious subjects, both for the feeling of vast space he gives to his background (the green plains and hills of Umbria) and for the composed grace of his figures and their immersion in the generally melancholic and mystical atmosphere created by the blending of chiaroscuro and deep color. This style was the starting point for the young Raphael.

Often, however, Perugino repeated himself, and the results are cold and only superficially devout; and after the famous frescoes of the Collegio del Cambio at Perugia (1500) his work began to decline. But the portrait of *Francesco delle Opere* (1494) in the Uffizi is justly renowned. Of the subject — a Florentine craftsman, carver of precious stones — we are shown head and shoulders, dignified in posture and set against the delicate and airy landscape in the background in a way that tends to idealize him. In this type of portrait there is probably a certain Flemish influence. The *Madonna and Child with John the Baptist and St. Sebastian* (1493), on the other hand, is a fine example of Perugino's religious paintings.

Lorenzo Costa, of Ferrarese origin, began work in the nervous style of Ercole de' Roberti, but later came under the influence of the much calmer Francia and Perugino. His *St. Sebastian* is a mature work, tranquil and even sentimental in the charming figure of the young boy.

▲
Perugino: Madonna and Child with Saints

▶
Lorenzo Costa: St. Sebastian

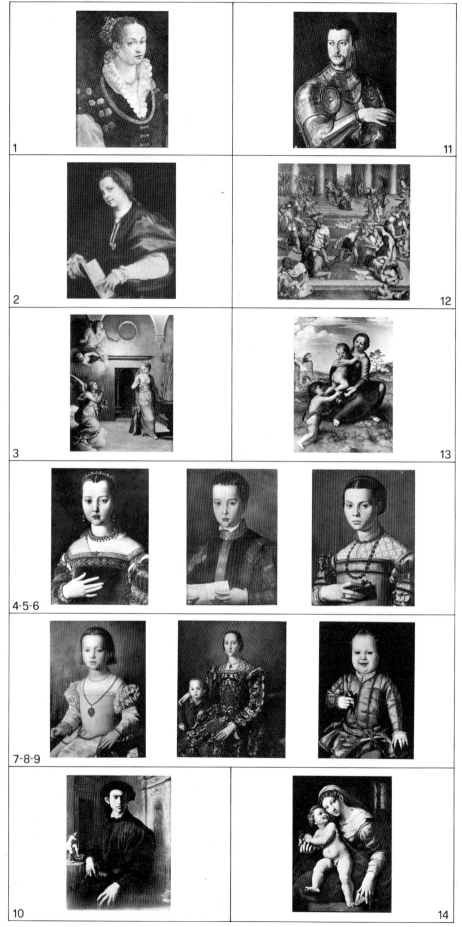

ALESSANDRO ALLORI (1535-1607)
1. **PORTRAIT OF BIANCA CAPPELLO (?)**
   (1500) Fresco on plaster; 0.69 × 0.48.

ANDREA DEL SARTO (1486-1531)
2. **PORTRAIT OF A YOUNG WOMAN**
   (783) Oil on wood; 0.87 × 0.69.

GIOVANNI BIZZELLI (1556-1622)
3. **ANNUNCIATION**
   (1547) Tempera on wood; 0.57 × 0.44.

AGNOLO BRONZINO (1503-1572)
4. **PORTRAIT OF MARIE DE' MEDICI**
   (1572) Tempera on wood; 0.52 × 0.38.
   Painted in 1553.
5. **PORTRAIT OF FRANESCO DE' MEDICI**
   (1571) Tempera on wood; 0.58 × 0.41.
   Painted in 1553.
6. **PORTRAIT OF GIRL WITH BOOK**
   (770) Tempera on wood; 0.58 × 0.46.
7. **PORTRAIT OF ISABELLA DE' MEDICI**
   (1472) Tempera on wood; 0.63 × 0.48.
8. **PORTRAIT OF ELEONORA OF TOLEDO
   WITH HER SON GIOVANNI DE' MEDICI**
   (748) Tempera on wood; 1.15 × 0.96.
9. **PORTRAIT OF GIOVANNI DE' MEDICI**
   (1475) Tempera on wood; 0.58 × 0.45.
10. **PORTRAIT OF YOUNG MAN IN BLACK**
    (1575) Tempera on wood; 0.98 × 0.82.
11. **PORTRAIT OF COSIMO I**
    (28 dep.) Tempera on wood; 0.74 × 0.58.

DANIELE DA VOLTERRA (c. 1509-1566)
12. **SLAUGHTER OF THE INNOCENTS**
    (1429) Tempera on wood; 1.47 × 1.44.

**FRANCESCO DI CRISTOFANO
CALLED FRANCIABIGIO** (1482-1525)
13. **MADONNA AND CHILD** with St. John
    (Madonna of the Well)
    (1445) Tempera on wood; 1.06 × 0.81.

GIULIO ROMANO (1492/99-1566)
14. **MADONNA AND CHILD**
    (217) Oil on wood; 1.02 × 0.78.

TRIBUNE OF BUONTALENTI

CECCHINO SALVIATI (1510-1563)
15. CHARITY
(2157) Oil on wood; 1.56 × 1.22.

AGNOLO BRONZINO (1503-1572)
16. PORTRAIT OF BARTOLOMEO PANCIATICHI
(741) Oil on wood; 1.04 × 0.85.
17. PORTRAIT OF LUCREZIA PANCIATICHI
(736) Oil on wood; 1.04 × 0.85.

JACOPO CARRUCCI CALLED PONTORMO (1494-1557)
18. PORTRAIT OF COSIMO THE ELDER
(3574) Oil on wood; 0.87 × 0.65.
19. EXPULSION FROM PARADISE
(1517) Oil on wood; 0.43 × 0.31.
20. LEDA AND THE SWAN
(1556) Oil on wood; 0.55 × 0.40.
21. CHARITY (Madonna and Child with Infant St. John)
(4347) Oil on wood; 0.89 × 0.74.

RAFFAELLO SANZIO (1483-1520)
22. YOUNG ST. JOHN THE BAPTIST
(1446) Oil on canvas; 1.65 × 1.47.
Raffaello's workshop.

RIDOLFO DEL GHIRLANDAIO
(1483-1561)
23. PORTRAIT OF A MAN
(2155) Oil on wood; 0.42 × 0.33.

ROSSO FIORENTINO (1495-1540)
24. MUSICAL ANGEL
(1505) Oil on wood; 0.39 × 0.47.

CECCHINO SALVIATI (1510-1563)
25. CHRIST CARRYING CROSS
(801) Oil on wood; 0.66 × 0.45.

GIORGIO VASARI (1511-1573)
26. POSTHUMOUS PORTRAIT OF LORENZO THE MAGNIFICENT
(1578) Oil on wood; 0.90 × 0.72.
27. IMMACULATE CONCEPTION
(1524) Oil on wood; 0.58 × 0.39.
28. A MIRACLE OF THE PROPHET ELIJAH
(1470) Oil on wood; 0.40 × 0.29.

The twenty eight paintings reproduced here have recently been returned to the Tribuna, where they were hung originally.

Mantegna: Adoration of the Magi

Andrea Mantegna was a great painter and the first Renaissance artist of Northern Italy. He was trained in Padua in the school of the antiquarian Squarcione, and was influenced also by the works of the Florentine Donatello in that city (the equestrian statue of Gattamelata and the high altar in the church of Sant'Antonio). His chief characteristics are a passionate love of antiquity, a vigorous sense of structure in figures and settings, an extreme technical mastery united with a profound moral severity and dignity. Mantegna left Padua to work at the court of the Gonzagas in Mantua, and from here his influence spread widely, to Verona, to Venice (in particular to Giovanni Bellini and the school of Murano), and to the school of Ferrara.

The triptych in the Uffizi — which has the *Adoration of the Magi* in the center and the *Ascension* and *Circumcision* at the sides — is known to have come from the collection of Don Antonio dei Medici, which in 1632 was united with the rest of the Medici collections. It therefore seems reasonable to date the work about 1466, the year in which Mantegna passed through Florence. Another hypothesis supposes that the three panels belonged to the more complex decorative scheme of a chapel in the Castle of Mantova, and came to Florence only later. In any case the triptych, extremely rich and exact in its detail and profoundly inventive, is on a level with Mantegna's best works.

The portrait, which is now presumed to be of Carlo dei Medici and to have been painted by Mantegna during his stay in Florence in 1466, was formerly held to be of the bishop Ludovico Gonzaga, and some critics have even considered it to be a sixteenth-century copy of an original by Mantegna. However, the high quality of this picture, with its disciplined structure, has convinced most scholars that it is in fact authentic.

This *St. Dominic* is a late work of Cosmè Tura, the great Ferrarese master who combined the brilliant clarity of Mantegna with the tormented, "expressionist" linear quality of Rogier van der Weyden. It originally belonged, together with other pieces (now in other collections) to a polyptych. The figure stands out firmly from the gold ground, but at the same time is defined and given character by line drawing, and the Saint is impressively portrayed in all his angry fervor.

▲

Cosmé Tura: St. Dominic, detail

▶

Mantegna: Cardinal Carlo dei Medici

GERMAN PAINTING OF THE RENAISSANCE

ALBRECHT DÜRER (1471-1528)
1. **PORTRAIT OF ARTIST'S FATHER**
(1086) Oil on wood; 0.47 × 0.39.
Signed and dated 1490.
2. **ADORATION OF THE MAGI**
(1434) Oil on wood; 1.00 × 1.14.
Signed and dated 1504.
3. **CALVARY**
(8406) Pen and Chiaroscuro on green paper
attached to wood; 0.58 × 0.40.
Signed and dated 1505.
4. **MADONNA AND CHILD**
(1171) Oil on wood; 0.43 × 0.31.
Signed and dated 1526.

FROM ALBRECHT DÜRER (HANS BALDUNG GRIEN?)
5. **ADAM**
(8433) Oil on wood; 2.12 × 0.85.
6. **EVE**
(8432) Oil on wood; 2.12 × 0.85.
Copies from the originals in the Prado,
dated 1507.

ALBRECHT DÜRER
7. **ST. PHILIP THE APOSTLE**
(1089) Oil on canvas; 0.45 × 0.38.
Signed and dated 1516.
8. **ST. JAMES THE APOSTLE**
(1099) Oil on canvas; 0.46 × 0.37.
Signed and dated 1516.

LUKAS CRANACH (1472-1553)
9. **ADAM**
(1459) Oil on wood; 1.72 × 0.63.
Signed and dated 1528.
10. **EVE**
(1458) Oil on wood; 1.67 × 0.61.
Part of number 9.
11. **SELF-PORTRAIT**
(1631) Oil on wood; 0.64 × 0.49.
Signed and dated 1550.
12. **ST. GEORGE SAVES THE PRINCESS FROM THE DRAGON**
(1056) Oil on wood; 0.19 × 0.18.

SCHOOL OF LUKAS CRANACH
13. **PORTRAIT OF A WOMAN**
(323 verdi) Oil on wood; 0.42 × 0.29.

LUKAS CRANACH (1472-1553)
14. **PORTRAIT OF MARTIN LUTHER**
(1160) Oil on wood; 0.37 × 0.23.
Signed and dated 1529.
15. **PORTRAIT OF LUTHER'S WIFE, CATHERINE BORE**
(1139) Oil on wood; 0.37 × 0.23.
Part of number 14.
16. **PORTRAIT OF MARTIN LUTHER**
(512) Oil on wood; 0.21 × 0.16.
Signed and dated 1543.
17. **PORTRAIT OF MELANCHTON**
(472) Oil on wood; 0.21 × 0.16.
Part of number 16.

WORKSHOP OF LUKAS CRANACH
18. **PORTRAIT OF FREDERICK III ELECTOR OF SAXONY**
(1150) Oil on wood; 0.20 × 0.15.
Signed (but work of workshop) and
dated 1533.
19. **PORTRAIT OF JOHN I ELECTOR OF SAXONY**
(1149) Oil on wood; 0.20 × 0.15.
Signed (but work of workshop) and
dated 1533.
Part of number 18.

GERMAN PAINTING OF THE RENAISSANCE

HANS VON KLUMBACH (1476? - 1522)
1. **STORIES OF SS. PETER AND PAUL: VOCATION OF ST. PETER**
   (1034) Oil on wood; 1.30 × 1.00.
2. **STORIES OF SS. PETER AND PAUL: CRUCIFIXION OF ST. PETER**
   (1030) Oil on wood; 1.30 × 1.00.
3. **STORIES OF SS. PETER AND PAUL: CONVERSION OF ST. PAUL**
   (1020) Oil on wood; 1.30 × 1.00
4. **STORIES OF SS. PETER AND PAUL: BEHEADING OF ST. PAUL**
   (1044) Oil on wood; 1.30 × 1.00.
   Other panels on display are:
   Sermon of St. Peter
   Liberation of St. Peter
   Capture of SS. Peter and Paul
   St. Paul Ascending into Heaven
   (1060-1047-1072-1058).
   Back; Four panels with the figures of
   SS. Peter and Paul.

GERMAN SCHOOL OF XVI CENTURY (HANS VON KLUMBACH?)
5. **CRUCIFIXION**
   (1025) Oil on wood; 1.67 × 0.92.

HANS BURGKMAIR (1473-1531)
6. **PORTRAIT OF A MAN**
   (432 P.) Oil on pergamen placed on wood; 0.32 × 0.27.
   Signed and dated 1506.

HANS MALER SCHWAZ (Early XVI Century)
7. **PORTRAIT OF FERDINAND OF CASTILE**
   (1215) Oil on wood; 0.33 × 0.23.
   Dated 1524.

HANS HOLBEIN (1497-1543)
8. **PORTRAIT OF SIR RICHARD SOUTHWELL**
   (1087) Oil on wood; 0.47 × 0.38.
   Dated 1536.

SCHOOL OF HANS HOLBEIN
9. **PORTRAIT OF A MAN** (Thomas Moore?)
   (1120) Oil on wood; 0.42 × 0.36.

JAN BRUEGEL (1568-1625)
10. **CALVARY**
    (1083) Oil on wood; 0.60 × 0.42.
11. **LANDSCAPE**
    (1179) Oil on copper; 0.37 × 0.25.

ALBRECHT ALTDORFER (c. 1480-1538)
12. **MARTYRDOM OF ST. FLORIAN**
    (4 dep.) Oil on wood; 0.76 × 0.67.
13. **ST. FLORIAN TAKING LEAVE OF MONASTERY**
    (5 dep.) Oil on wood; 0.81 × 0.67.

Dürer: Adoration of the Magi, detail

Dürer was never in Florence, though some scholars have believed he was, and though he came in 1506 as near as Bologna. However, the presence in the Uffizi of works by this great German master, due principally to an advantageous exchange of paintings with Vienna in 1792, has also a historical justification. Through his famous engravings, Dürer exercised considerable influence over the Florentine painters of the early sixteenth century. This is particularly plain in the case of Pontormo, who at one stage of his career modeled his work entirely on Dürer.

Dürer (1471-1528) was a pupil of Wohlgemut in Nuremberg, then came under the influence of Schongauer, and subsequently evolved his powerful and patiently detailed style through wide research. Journeys played an important part in his growth: from 1490-94 he travelled in Germany, in 1494-95 he was in Venice, in 1505-06 he came again to Italy and especially Venice, and in 1519 he was in the Netherlands. Gothic and Nordic elements (evident particularly in his admirable engravings) thus fused in his work with a sense of structure and a pictorial richness learned from the southern Renaissance.

The *Portrait of the Artist's Father* goes back to 1490, and is in fact the first of Dürer's known works, painted when he was nineteen and about to leave Nuremberg for his first long educational journey. Perhaps he wanted to take with him his parents' likenesses. This painting is of Flemish type, but lively and strong in structure. The *Adoration of the Magi* (once part of a triptych) was painted in 1504 for the church of Wittenberg Castle, and is a mature and very impressive work, in which the influence of Italian artists, especially Mantegna and Giovanni Bellini, is evident in the rigorously correct spatial structure of the ruins, in the monumentality of the figures, and in the clear and subtle colors. But only Dürer himself could have given the work its full-blooded expressive vigor and its immensely romantic, imaginative spirit.

Hans Holbein (1497-1543) was from Augsburg, spent also some time in Italy, and then (from 1526 on) worked in England, where he won great fame with his portraits (he was the court painter of Henry VIII). The Uffizi has one of the finest portraits of his English period, that of the diplomat *Sir Richard Southwell*, dated 1536. It has a concentrated clarity which brings out also the character of the subject, and a dignity similar to that of the portraits of his contemporary, Bronzino.

▶

Holbein: Portrait of Richard Southwell

Dürer: Portrait of the Artist's Father

DUTCH AND FLEMISH PAINTING OF THE RENAISSANCE

MASTER OF HOOGSTRAETEN
(active c. 1490-1520)
1. **MADONNA ENTHRONED WITH SS. CATHERINE AND BARBARA**
(1019) Oil on wood; 0.87 × 0.73.

MASTER OF VIRGO INTER VIRGINES
(active c. 1460-1520)
2. **CRUCIFIXION**
(1237) Oil on wood; 0.57 × 0.47.

GERARD DAVID (c. 1460-1520)
3. **ADORATION OF THE MAGI**
(1029) Oil on canvas; 0.95 × 0.80.
4. **DEPOSITION**
(1152) Oil on wood; 0.20 × 0.14.

JOOS VAN CLEVE (c. 1485-1540)
5. **PORTRAIT OF UNKNOWN MAN**
(1643) Oil on wood; 0.57 × 0.42.
6. **PORTRAIT OF MAN'S WIFE**
(1644) Oil on wood; 0.57 × 0.42.
7. **PORTRAIT OF A MAN**
(1645) Oil on wood; 0.31 × 0.20.

BERNAERT VAN ORLEY
(1492/95-1542)
8. **PORTRAIT OF UNKNOWN MAN**
(1140) Oil on wood; 0.37 × 0.29.
9. **PORTRAIT OF MAN'S WIFE**
(1161) Oil on wood; 0.37 × 0.29.

JOOS VAN CLEVE (c. 1485-1540)
10. **MATER DOLOROSA**
(1084) Oil on wood; 0.55 × 0.33.

QUINTEN MASSYS (1466-1530)
11. **ST. JEROME**
(1092) Oil on wood; 0.35 × 0.20.

HERRIMET DE BLES CALLED IL CIVETTA
12. **COPPER MINE**
(1051) Oil on wood; 0.83 × 1.13.

VENETIAN PAINTING OF THE XV CENTURY

ANDREA MANTEGNA (1431-1506)
1. **MADONNA AND CHILD**
   (Madonna of the Cave)
   (1348) Tempera on wood; 0.32 × 0.30.
2. **ASCENSION**
   (910) Tempera on wood; 0.86 × 0.43.
3. **ADORATION OF THE MAGI**
   (910) Tempera on wood; 0.77 × 0.75.
4. **CIRCUMCISION**
   (910) Tempera on wood; 0.86 × 0.43.
5. **PORTRAIT OF CARDINAL**
   CARLO DE' MEDICI (?)
   (8540) Tempera on wood; 0.41 × 0.30.

COSMÈ TURA (1432-1495)
6. **ST. DOMENIC**
   (3273) Tempera on wood; 0.51 × 0.32.
   Part of dismembered Polyptych; late work.

BARTOLOMEO VIVARINI (active 1450-1499)
7. **ST. LUDOVIC OF TOULOUSE**
   (3346) Tempera on wood; 0.68 × 0.36.

GIOVANNI BELLINI (c. 1430-1516)
8. **ALLEGORY**
   (631) Oil on wood; 0.73 × 1.19.
9. **LAMENTATION OVER THE BODY**
   OF CHRIST
   (943) Oil on wood; 0.76 × 1.21.
10. **PORTRAIT OF A GENTLEMAN**
    (1863) Oil on wood; 0.31 × 0.26.
    Work authentic, signature probably false.

CIMA DA CONEGLIANO (c. 1459-1518)
11. **MADONNA AND CHILD**
    (902) Oil on wood; 0.69 × 0.56.

VITTORE CARPACCIO
(c. 1455 - c. 1525)
12. **WARRIORS AND OLD MEN**
    (901) Oil on canvas; 0.68 × 0.42.
    Fragment of Crucifixion.

GIORGIONE (1478-1511)
13. **WARRIOR WITH EQUERRY**
    (Il Gattamelata)
    (911) Oil on canvas; 0.90 × 0.73.
    Attributed.
14. **MOSES UNDERGOING TRIAL BY FIRE**
    IN FRONT OF THE PHAROH
    (945) Mixed materials on wood; 0.90 × 0.72.
    Painted in collaboration.
15. **THE JUSTICE OF SALOMON**
    (947) Mixed materials on wood; 0.89 × 0.72
    Painted in collaboration.

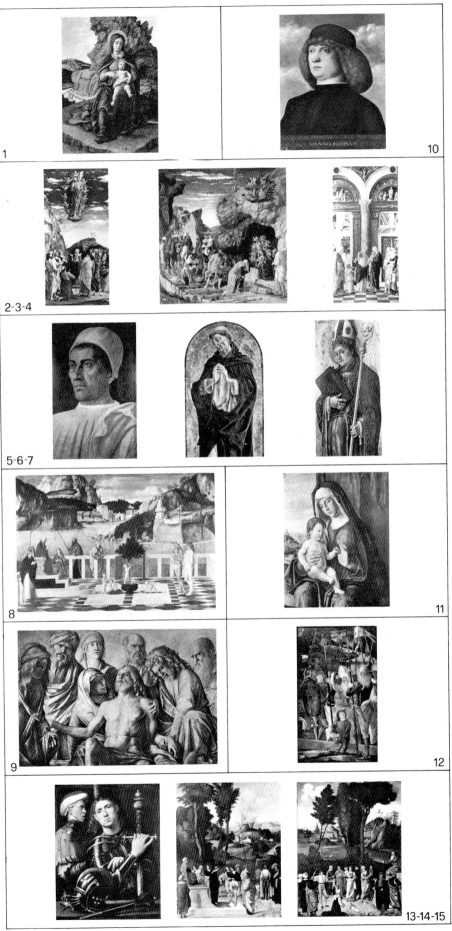

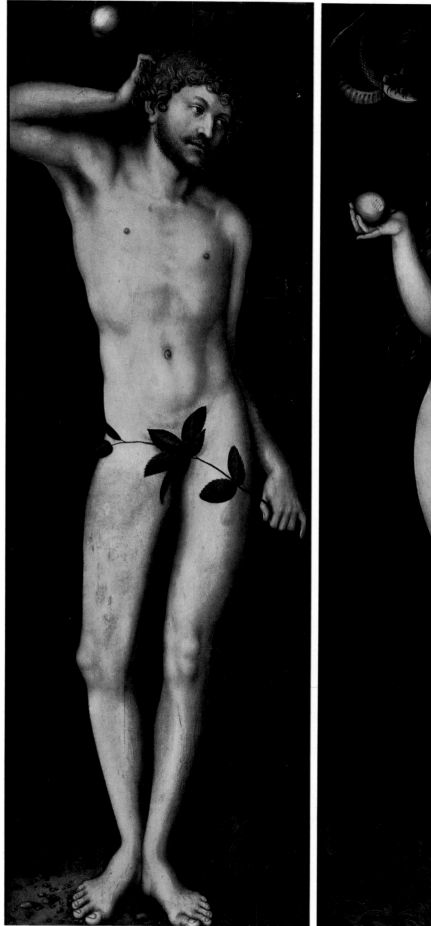

76

Cranach: Adam and Eve

Altdorfer: Story of St. Florian

Lukas Cranach (1472-1553) was of the same generation as Dürer, but there is in his work a subtle elegance anticipating Mannerism. His painting, as a result, has little moral depth, nor is it greatly concerned with matters of style, as is Dürer's. It is instead pleasing, refined in idiom, directed towards a vast clientèle satisfied with sensuous images of Venus, Lucretia, noble ladies, and allegorical themes.

In the *Adam and Eve* (1528) in the Uffizi, the same subject that had led Dürer to seek for the laws of harmony on which human beauty is based, becomes the inspiration for two slightly lascivious nudes, though the style is tense, and the figures have real grace.

By contrast the painting of Albrecht Altdorfer (c. 1480-1538), a master of the so-called "Danube School", is

strongly romantic. He creates spacious landscapes and fantastic settings for his figures. His *Stories of St. Florian* — which were painted, together with other panels now in Germany, for a church in Linz — are sufficient to give us an impression of his imaginative power. His unusual use of color helps to create a visionary atmosphere.

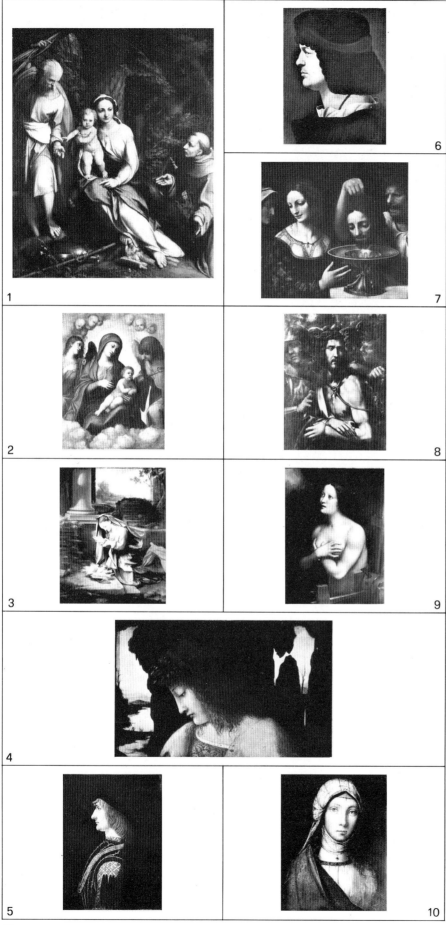

CORREGGIO AND LEONARDESQUE PAINTING OF CENTRAL ITALY

CORREGGIO (1489-1534)
1. **REST ON THE FLIGHT INTO EGYPT**
   (1455) Oil on canvas; 1.23×1.06.
2. **MADONNA AND CHILD IN GLORY**
   (1329) Oil on wood; 0.20×0.16.
3. **ADORATION OF THE CHILD**
   (1453) Oil on canvas; 0.81×0.67.

GIOVANNI ANTONIO BOLTRAFFIO (1467-1516)
4. **NARCISSUS**
   (2184) Oil on wood; 0.19×0.31.

GIOVANNI AMBROGIO DE PREDIS (1467-1517)
5. **PORTRAIT OF A MAN**
   (1494) Oil on wood; 0.60×0.45.

BERNARDINO DE CONTI (1450-1525?)
6. **PORTRAIT OF A MAN**
   (1883) Oil on wood; 0.42×0.32.

BERNARDINO LUINI (1475/80-1531/32)
7. **EXECUTIONER WITH THE HEAD OF JOHN THE BAPTIST**
   (1454) Oil on wood; 0.51×0.58.

GIOVANNI ANTONIO BAZZI CALLED IL SODOMA (1477-1549)
8. **CHRIST AT THE COLUMN**
   (738) Oil on wood; 0.85×0.60.

GIAMPIETRINO (First Half of XVI Century)
9. **ST. CATHERINE**
   (8544) Oil on wood; 0.64×0.50.

BOCCACCIO BOCCACINO (1467-1524)
10. **GYPSY**
    (8539) Oil on wood; 0.24×0.19.

78

EARLY XVI CENTURY PAINTING IN FLORENCE

MICHELANGELO BUONARROTI
(1475-1564)
1. **HOLY FAMILY (Tondo Doni)**
   (1456) Tempera on wood; tondo: diameter 1.20.

RAFFAELLO SANZIO (1483-1520)
2. **MADONNA AND CHILD WITH YOUNG ST. JOHN (Madonna del Cardellino)**
   (1447) Oil on wood; 1.07 × 0.77.
3. **PORTRAIT OF LEO X with Cardinals Giulio de' Medici and Luigi de' Rossi**
   (40 P) Oil on wood; 1.54 × 1.19.
4. **PORTRAIT OF PERUGINO**
   (1482) Oil on wood; 0.59 × 0.46. Attributed.
5. **PORTRAIT OF FRANCESCO MARIA DELLA ROVERE**
   (8760) Oil on wood; 0.47 × 0.35.
6. **PORTRAIT OF JULIUS II**
   (1450) Oil on wood; 1.07 × 0.80. Copy of the original.
7. **SELF-PORTRAIT**
   (1706) Oil on wood; 0.30 × 0.25. Attributed.
8. **PORTRAIT OF GUIDOBALDO DA MONTEFELTRO**
   (8538) Oil on wood; 0.69 × 0.52. Attributed.
9. **PORTRAIT OF ELISABETTA GONZAGA**
   (1441) Oil on wood; 0.58 × 0.36. Attributed.

MARIOTTO ALBERTINELLI
(1474-1515)
10. **VISITATION**
    (1587) Oil on wood; 2.35 × 1.50.
11. **PREDELLA OF VISITATION: ANNUNCIATION**
    (1586) Oil on wood; 0.23 × 1.50.
12. **PREDELLA OF VISITATION: NATIVITY**
    (1586) Oil on wood; 0.23 × 1.50.
13. **PREDELLA OF VISITATION: PRESENTATION AT THE TEMPLE**
    (1586) Oil on wood; 0.23 × 1.50.

GIULIANO BUGIARDINI (1475-1554)
14. **PORTRAIT OF A WOMAN**
    (8380) Oil on wood; 0.62 × 0.46.

FRANCESCO GRANACCI (1477-1543)
15. **JOSEPH PRESENTS THE PHAROH TO HIS FATHER AND BROTHERS**
    (2152) Oil on wood; 0.95 × 2.24.

AGNOLO BRONZINO (1503-1572)
16. **HOLY FAMILY with Young St. John**
    (8377) Oil on wood; 1.17 × 0.89. Signed.
17. **DEAD CHRIST WITH VIRGIN AND MARY MAGDALEN**
    (8545) Oil on wood; 1.05 × 1.00.

1-2-3

4-5-6

7-8-9

10

14

11-12-13

15-16-17

What is meant by "Venetian painting" originated with Giovanni Bellini (1435-1516), who during his very long career worked first alongside his brother-in-law Mantegna, then assimilated the innovations of Piero della Francesca and Antonello da Messina, and finally, as an old man, could hold his own worthily beside Giorgione and the young Titian. Perspective structure, harmony of spatial and volumetrical relationships, strong composition and incisive drawing, coloring and light effects, are all important in his work; though the main unifying elements are his sense of tonal values and his calm and contemplative spirit, which creates a sense of the brotherhood of all the things he represents. The Flemish van Eyck had already achieved this effect, but Bellini added to it the idealistic, Humanistic spirit of the Italian Renaissance.

The unique iconography of the *Allegory* in the Uffizi (formerly attributed to Giorgione) has given rise to much searching for explanations. It was once supposed that the source was a fourteenth-century French poem by Guillame de Deguilleville, "Le pelerinage de l'âme", but this idea has been rejected; other interpretations have been an allegory of Mercy or Justice, or a representation of Paradise. The Madonna is seated — in an enclosure with rich marble paving — on a throne between two saints, while beyond the parapet are St. Paul and St. Joseph watching the seated Child, to whom three putti are offering oranges. On the right are St. Job and St. Sebastian, and in the background a stupendous imaginary landscape, with a lake between steep hills and a glimpse of a village. The chromatic values of the scene are already similar to Giorgione's, although this work is dated around 1485, close to the *San Giobbe Altarpiece* in Venice. The painting was acquired in an exchange with the Imperial galleries of Vienna in 1793, which we owe to Abbot Lanzi. It was Cavalcaselle who attributed it to Bellini, and Berenson who first gave it an exact date.

Giovanni Bellini: Allegory

ANDREA DEL SARTO (1486-1531)
1. **MADONNA OF THE HARPIES**
   (Madonna and Child Enthroned with
   SS. Francis and John the Evangelist)
   (1577) Oil on wood; 2.07 × 1.78.
   Signed and dated 1517.
2. **ALTARPIECE OF FOUR SAINTS**
   (SS. Michael, John Gualberto, John the Baptis
   and Bernardo of the Uberti):
   Predella with four stories one for each Saint
   (8395, 8396) Oil on wood; Altarpiece:
   1.86 × 1.75; Predella: 0.21 × 1.83 each.
3. **ST. JAMES AND TWO BOYS**
   (1583) Oil on canvas; Banner: 1.56 × 0.85.

**FRANCESCO UBERTINI CALLED
IL BACHIACCA** (c. 1494-1557)
4. **DEPOSITION**
   (511) Oil on wood; 0.93 × 0.71.
5. **PREDELLA PANEL: A STORY
   OF ST. ACACIO (Baptism)**
   (877) Oil on wood; 0.38 × 2.52.
6. **PREDELLA PANEL: A STORY
   OF ST. ACACIO (Battle Scene)**
   (877) Oil on wood; 0.38 × 2.52.
7. **PREDELLA PANEL: A STORY OF
   ST. ACACIO**
   (877) Oil on wood; 0.38 × 2.52.
8. **CHRIST AND CAIAPHAS**
   (8407) Oil on wood; 0.50 × 0.41.
9. **TOBIAS AND THE ANGEL**
   (4336) Oil on wood; 0.31 × 0.25.

ALONSO BERRUGUETE (c. 1486-1561)
10. **SALOME**
    (5274) Oil on wood; 0.88 × 0.71.
11. **MADONNA AND CHILD**
    (5852) Oil on wood; 0.84 × 0.61.

DOMENICO BECCAFUMI (1486-1551)
12. **HOLY FAMILY**
    (780) Oil on wood; tondo; diameter: 0.84.

GIORGIO VASARI (1511-1574)
13. **ADORATION OF THE SHEPHERDS**
    (9449) Oil on wood; 0.89 × 0.67.

MANNERISM IN FLORENCE

ROSSO FIORENTINO (1495-1540)
1. **MADONNA AND CHILD ENTHRONED** with SS. John the Baptist, Anthony Abbot, Stephen and Jerome
   (3190) Tempera on wood; 1.72 × 1.41.
2. **MOSES DEFENDING THE DAUGHTERS OF JETHRO**
   (2151) Oil on canvas; 1.60 × 1.17.
3. **PORTRAIT OF YOUNG GIRL**
   (3245) Tempera on wood; 0.45 × 0.33.

JACOPO CARRUCCI CALLED PONTORMO (1494-1557)
4. **PORTRAIT OF WOMAN WITH BASKET OF SPINDLES**
   (1480) Oil on wood; 0.76 × 0.54.
5. **PORTRAIT OF THE MUSICIAN FRANCESCO DELL'AJOLLE**
   (743) Oil on wood; 0.88 × 0.67.
6. **SUPPER AT EMMAUS**
   (8740) Oil on wood; 2.30 × 1.75.
   Painted in 1525.
7. **MARTYRDOM OF ST. MAURICE AND THE THEBAN LEGION**
   (1525) Oil on wood; 0.66 × 0.45.
8. **BIRTH OF JOHN THE BAPTIST**
   (1532) Oil on wood; diameter: 0.54.
9. **ST. ANTHONY ABBOT**
   (8379) Oil on canvas; 0.79 × 0.66.
10. **MADONNA AND CHILD ENTHRONED WITH SS. JEROME AND FRANCIS**
    (1538) Tempera on wood; 0.73 × 0.61.
11. **PORTRAIT OF MARIA SALVIATI (?)**
    (3565) Oil on wood; 0.87 × 0.71.

JACOPINO DEL CONTE (1510-1598)
12. **MADONNA AND CHILD WITH YOUNG ST. JOHN**
    (6009) Oil on wood; 1.26 × 0.94.

FRANCIABIGIO (1482-1525)
13. **PORTRAIT OF A YOUNG MAN WITH GLOVES**
    (8381) Oil on wood; 0.58 × 0.45.

DOMENICO PULIGO (1492-1527)
14. **PORTRAIT OF PIETRO CARNESECCHI**
    (1489) Oil on wood; 0.59 × 0.39.

1

9

2

10

3-4-5

6

11

7

12

8

13-14

The work of Giorgione (1477-1510) represents a development in tonal painting with the addition of the *sfumato* element developed by Leonardo, and a deepening of poetic significance. He creates mysterious and evocative atmospheres, in an idiom which has affinities with music. The two panel paintings in the Uffizi — the *Judgment of Solomon* and the *Trial of Moses* — are youthful works which show signs of collaboration in the figures (especially in the *Judgment of Solomon*), but the deep and spacious landscapes, almost more important than the human figures, are by Giorgione himself. The portrait of a *Knight and his Squire*, called Gattamelata, has once again been attributed to Giorgione (his authorship was doubted for a time, Cavazzola among others being suggested as the true author), but the attribution is still not certain. In any case it is a fine composition, with the armor in the foreground forming a still life, and the high quality of the painting and romantic atmosphere relate it closely to the later works of Giorgione.

Correggio (1489-1534) also started out from the premises of Leonardo to contribute to Italian painting new compositional schemes — diagonal structures or grand choral visions. His figures are monumental but more human and milder, and he has a delicate grace, almost feminine, expressed in sweetly flowing lines and intense, harmonious colors. He opened up possibilities that were to be developed by Baroque painters, especially in the eighteenth century. The *Adoration of the Child* in the Uffizi is a typical — and very popular — masterpiece, of a sensuous tenderness which comes close to sentimentality. The Madonna is portrayed in contemplation of her Son, who is lying on the straw and brightly lit, while the rest of the scene is almost in twilight. The classical column gives a note of nobility to the setting, which for the rest is humble and ordinary, while in the background there is a magnificent glimpse of landscape. Thus the typical Leonardesque elements (the sweetness and grace of the figures, the twilight atmosphere, the cosmic vastness of the background) are transformed to produce intensely emotional effects and a certain sentimental softness.

▲
Giorgione: A Knight and his Squire
◄
Giorgione: Judgment of Solomon, detail

Correggio: Adoration of the Child

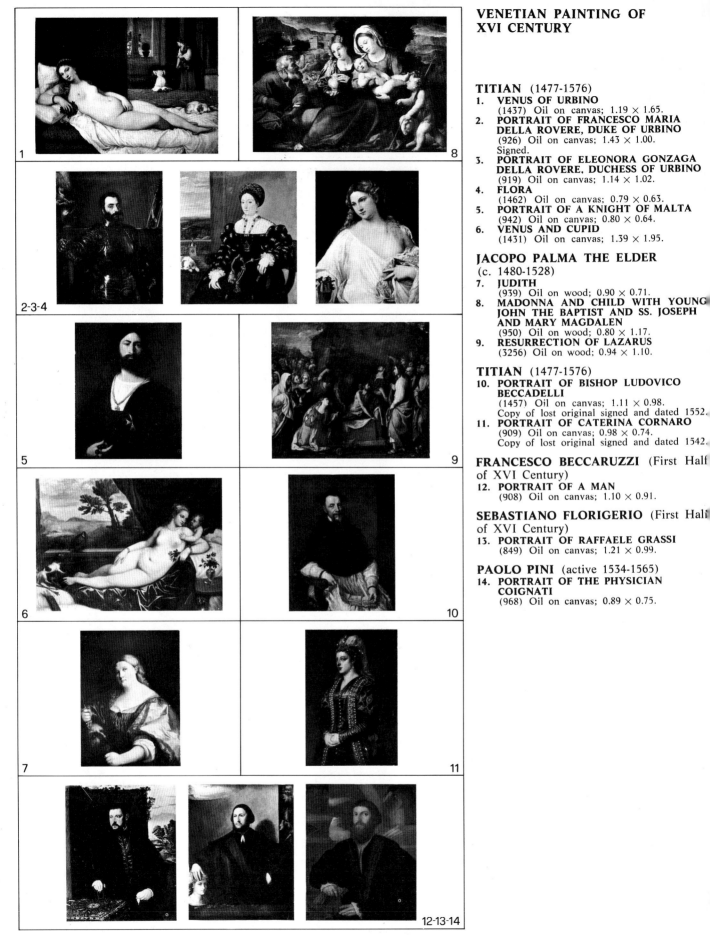

VENETIAN PAINTING OF XVI CENTURY

TITIAN (1477-1576)
1. **VENUS OF URBINO**
   (1437) Oil on canvas; 1.19 × 1.65.
2. **PORTRAIT OF FRANCESCO MARIA DELLA ROVERE, DUKE OF URBINO**
   (926) Oil on canvas; 1.43 × 1.00. Signed.
3. **PORTRAIT OF ELEONORA GONZAGA DELLA ROVERE, DUCHESS OF URBINO**
   (919) Oil on canvas; 1.14 × 1.02.
4. **FLORA**
   (1462) Oil on canvas; 0.79 × 0.63.
5. **PORTRAIT OF A KNIGHT OF MALTA**
   (942) Oil on canvas; 0.80 × 0.64.
6. **VENUS AND CUPID**
   (1431) Oil on canvas; 1.39 × 1.95.

JACOPO PALMA THE ELDER
(c. 1480-1528)
7. **JUDITH**
   (939) Oil on wood; 0.90 × 0.71.
8. **MADONNA AND CHILD WITH YOUNG JOHN THE BAPTIST AND SS. JOSEPH AND MARY MAGDALEN**
   (950) Oil on wood; 0.80 × 1.17.
9. **RESURRECTION OF LAZARUS**
   (3256) Oil on wood; 0.94 × 1.10.

TITIAN (1477-1576)
10. **PORTRAIT OF BISHOP LUDOVICO BECCADELLI**
    (1457) Oil on canvas; 1.11 × 0.98.
    Copy of lost original signed and dated 1552.
11. **PORTRAIT OF CATERINA CORNARO**
    (909) Oil on canvas; 0.98 × 0.74.
    Copy of lost original signed and dated 1542.

FRANCESCO BECCARUZZI (First Half of XVI Century)
12. **PORTRAIT OF A MAN**
    (908) Oil on canvas; 1.10 × 0.91.

SEBASTIANO FLORIGERIO (First Half of XVI Century)
13. **PORTRAIT OF RAFFAELE GRASSI**
    (849) Oil on canvas; 1.21 × 0.99.

PAOLO PINI (active 1534-1565)
14. **PORTRAIT OF THE PHYSICIAN COIGNATI**
    (968) Oil on canvas; 0.89 × 0.75.

EMILIAN PAINTING OF XVI CENTURY

PARMIGIANINO (1505-1540)
1. **MADONNA OF THE LONG NECK**
   (230 P) 2.16 × 1.32.
2. **MADONNA OF ST. ZACHARY** (Madonna and Child with SS. Zachary, Mary Magdalen
   (1328) Oil on wood; 0.73 × 0.60.
3. **PORTRAIT OF A MAN**
   (1623) Oil on wood; 1.00 × 0.70.

NICCOLÒ DELL'ABATE (1509-1571)
4. **PORTRAIT OF YOUNG MAN WITH CAP**
   (1377) Oil on wood; 0.47 × 0.41.
   Attributed.

LUDOVICO MAZZOLINO
(c. 1479-1528?)
5. **SLAUGHTER OF THE INNOCENTS**
   (1350) Oil on wood; 0.39 × 0.59.
6. **CIRCUMCISION**
   (1355) Oil on wood; 0.40 × 0.29.
7. **MADONNA AND CHILD WITH SS. Anne, John the Evangelist and Zachary** (Madonna and St. Anne of the Cherries)
   (1347) Oil on wood; 0.33 × 0.29.
8. **ADORATION OF THE CHILD**
   (1352) Oil on wood; 0.79 × 0.60.

AMICO ASPERTINI (c. 1475-1552)
9. **ADORATION OF THE SHEPHERDS**
   (3803) Oil on wood; 0.44 × 0.34.

NICCOLÒ PISANO (First Half of XVI Century)
10. **MADONNA AND CHILD WITH YOUNG ST. JOHN**
    (3543) Oil on wood; 0.62 × 0.50.

BENVENUTO TISI CALLED IL GAROFALO (1481-1559)
11. **CHRIST AND TRIBUTE MONEY**
    (1353) Oil on wood; 0.20 × 0.22.
    Copy of a painting by Titian.
12. **ANNUNCIATION**
    (1365) Oil on wood; 0.55 × 0.76.

GIROLAMO DA CARPI (1501-1556)
13. **MARY AND MARTHA BEFORE CHRIST**
    (354) Oil on wood; 0.39 × 0.50.
14. **ADORATION OF THE CHILD**
    (114 P) Oil on wood; 0.85 × 1.08.

LAVINIA FONTANA (1552-1614)
15. **NOLI ME TANGERE**
    (383) Oil on canvas; 0.81 × 0.65.

IPPOLITO SCARSELLA CALLED LO SCARSELLINO (1551-1620)
16. **JUDGEMENT OF PARIS**
    (1382) Oil on copper; 0.50 × 0.72.

1-2-3

4

12

5

13

6-7-8

9-10-11

14-15-16

Michelangelo: Holy Family

Arguing against Leonardo, Michelangelo asserted the superiority of sculpture over painting, conceiving the latter also as a vigorous plastic art, intended to embody moral ideas rather than to imitate the phenomena of the natural world.

Painted in 1504-05 on the occasion of the marriage of Angelo Doni with Maddalena Strozzi, the *Holy Family* in the Uffizi is in fact a powerful and sculptural composition in which the group of figures — Madonna, Child, and St. Joseph — seem to be carved in spiral form from a single block, given force by the prominent muscles,

and pervaded by a kind of severe pathos, of heroic mold. The nude figures in the background form a sort of parapet beyond which a landscape is barely outlined, so that our vision is concentrated in the foreground, on the holy group with its extraordinary tension. The abstract but vibrant color, to which the light gives changing reflections, adds to the strength of the portrayal. These innovations were the starting point for the new Mannerist artists, with their insistence on anatomy, their complex and far-fetched concepts of form, their anti-naturalistic, intellectual disposition.

88

Raphael was in Florence between 1504 and 1508, and during this period he progressed from his earliest style, based on that of Perugino, to one influenced by the discoveries of Leonardo and Michelangelo, but also by the simple Classicism of Fra' Bartolomeo.

In the various Madonnas of these years, such as the *Madonna of the Goldfinch* (fig. 90) — painted for Lorenzo Nasi in about 1506 — the pyramidal, several-figured compositions have a calm, rhythmical quality quite different from both the subtle and vibrant complexity of Leonardo and the extraordinary tension of Michelangelo. Buxom and serene, Raphael's figures group together with a sense of measured harmony, and the spacious and gentle hilly landscape marked by a few slender trees of Umbrian type forms a fitting background to them. A sense of surrounding harmony relates landscape and figures. The two charming children are observing each other with a naturalness which reveals the artist's attention to infant behavior, and the Virgin has stopped reading for a moment to watch them. In the drawing, gently curving lines and oval forms are dominant; and the solid modeling is softened by shading of Leonardesque type. The surface chiaroscuro unites with the warm but controlled color in the "saturated compactness of local, still Umbrian tones".

Raphael: Portrait of Leo X

Already when he was in Florence Raphael had applied himself to the portrait, achieving — in those of *Angelo* and *Maddalena Doni*, in the Pitti Palace — a solemn dignity entirely of the sixteenth century. But when he painted the *Portrait of Leo X* with two cardinals — in Rome, about 1518-19 — he had reached his full maturity, and was capable of synthesizing all the pictorial possibilities of the epoch, including Venetian coloring.

The great Florentine Pope (Giovanni dei Medici) dominates the painting, with the cardinals Giulio dei Medici and Luigi dei Rossi standing a little behind him; but the pictorial context, rather than isolating the figure, unites it with the setting, and thus adds to its strength. The superb still-life of the illuminated book and the finely wrought bell on the red velvet-covered table, as well as the formal dignity of the figure of the Pope himself and the triumphal red tones of the whole, contributes to defining the Humanistic and hedonistic personality of the man, and his nobility. There is even a display of virtuosity in the depiction of the chairback, with the "burnished gold ball in which as in a mirror the light from the windows, the Pope's shoulders, and the surrounding room are reflected" (Vasari).

Full of a sense of confidence in the course of history, in the imperious but self-contained image of Leo X, this masterpiece is also an assured affirmation of the enormous possibilities of paint. In the fabrics alone there are many sumptuous variations of color tone and of texture (damask, velvet, satin); and of the pictorial space it has been said that it is already Baroque, or rather that it shows, carried to its furthest extreme, "the dominion of Classicist form over a world of color and sensation" (Ortolani).

Florence in the early sixteenth century was not only the place of work for a few years of great geniuses like Leonardo, Michelangelo and Raphael, but also, for a longer period, the home of a not outstanding but still appreciable school of Classicist painters. Fra Bartolomeo, for example, with his severe religious spirit, achieves a noble monumentality which influenced Raphael, and his heavy chiaroscuro has a quality learned from the *sfumato* of Leonardo. The work of Mariotto Albertinelli (1474-1515) is similar to Fra Bartolomeo's, but distinguished by a more Flemish use of enamel-like colors. In his *Visitation* we can see how the Peruginesque style he set out from is surpassed in a calm and truthful but still imposing simplicity. The arch formed by the two figures, for example, is repeated and magnified by the arch in the loggia in the background. The chromatic values of the painting, besides, can stand comparison even with the Venetian of the same period (the altarpiece is from 1503).

But the most complete of these artists is certainly Andrea del Sarto (1486-1531), whose technical perfection Vasari recognized so far as to call him "without error", although he goes on, justifiably, to criticize him for "a certain timidity of spirit". He is an excellent draftsman, capable in his frescoes and altarpieces of creating ambitious compositions, and gifted if not brilliant as a colorist. He has a fine and sometimes very subtle sensitivity, which is evident also in his portraits. Typical is the portrait of an unknown *Young Woman*, who is pointing with a slightly teasing expression to a book with a sonnet of Petrarch ("Go warm sighs to the cold heart"). Although the bold form introduced to portraiture by Raphael has been adhered to, this figure is enlivened by a more natural grace. This effect is enhanced by the warm color, with its play of lights and shadows, which emphasizes the fullness of the form but at the same time softens it. The tone of the whole is thus of familiarity, but also of a lyrical delicacy. The portrait was placed in the Tribune of the Uffizi as early as 1589.

▲
Albertinelli: Visitation, detail

▶
Andrea del Sarto: Portrait of a Young Woman

◀
Raphael: Madonna of the Goldfinch

Titian: Venus of Urbino

A different sort of Classicism from that of Central Italy (based above all on "drawing") was being developed at the same time in the Venetian area, thanks to the genius of Titian (1477-1576), who during his extremely long working life achieved international fame. Starting from the premises of Giovanni Bellini and Giorgione (from whom in a certain phase he is almost indistinguishable), he gradually developed a personal style more intense in composition and color, a more impetuous self-confidence and a more passionate, instinctive eloquence. While Giorgione is a Romantic, Titian has in fact the robust strength of a Classic. In the *Assumption of the Virgin* in the church of the Frari, Venice (1518), he went on to develop a monumentality of Roman scope, based, however, not only on majestic structure and dramatic action, but also on the chromatic strength of tonally constructed light. And even when (a little after 1540) Titian came under the influence of Mannerism and its constrictions he was always saved by his great pictorial talents, which in his last period allowed him to achieve a daring style in which form has begun to disintegrate, leaving only the creative magic of his brush.

92

The *Venus of Urbino* (called after the town it comes from) was painted in 1538 for Duke Guidobaldo II of Urbino, and is one of the masterpieces of Titian's maturity. The unashamedly sensual naked body of the Venus dominates the foreground of the painting, her gold-tinted flesh contrasting with the white sheet and the green curtain behind her, while the bright note of color in the flowers she is holding is echoed by the red of the cushions. But on the right we see deep into the room, where are the lively figures of two maids intent on looking for clothes in chests; and beyond an open window the light of the evening sky gives a sense of greater spaciousness to the interior. Thus a balance is created between the intimate warmth of the alcove on the left side and the spatial depth and more subtle atmosphere of the scene on the right, which adds to the fascination of the painting, triumphantly yet serenely sensual.

Titian was also a great portraitist. In 1536-37 he painted the Duke and Duchess of Urbino, *Francesco Maria della Rovere* and *Eleonora Gonzaga*, but these portraits have a certain academic sedateness which prevent his talents from showing to their best advantage.

The *Flora*, however, from the end of Titian's first phase (c. 1515), is a justly famous work. It still shows signs of the influence of Giorgione, being in spirit between romantic and sensuous; but it has a richer breadth of form and a more exultant intensity of color, revealing the already distinct personality of Titian.

Palma il Vecchio reflects in his rich and serene style, though on a more modest level, the characteristics of the early work of Titian.

▲
Titian: The Duchess of Urbino

▶
Titian: Flora

◀
Palma il Vecchio: Judith

At the end of the second decade of the sixteenth century there occured in Florence the first clear manifestations of the fanciful, sophistic, restless spirit, the intellectual reaction to Classicism — although based on the highest achievements of the Classicists, especially Michelangelo — that led to the style now known as Mannerism (and which still today is cause for much debate).

This tendency is represented by two great figures, Pontormo and Rosso Fiorentino, though as personalities they were entirely different. Pontormo (1494-1556) was in fact introverted and melancholy, and is difficult to follow in his development. He made sudden jumps from one style to another; from a first stage under the influence of Andrea del Sarto to a next dominated by the foreign, Nordic art of Dürer, to an attempt, finally to emulate the tense strength of Michelangelo, in which he failed. His continuous and ever more personal experimentation led to his being little undersood or appreciated. Rosso (1495-1540), on the other hand, was extrovert, spirited and ironic, intellectual and cultured but at the same time instinctive. He attempted to resolve by essentially pictorial means the traditional Florentine dualism of form and color, in which drawing came first and color later as an addition.

In Pontormo's *Supper at Emmaus* (from the Certosa of Galluzzo, dated 1525), the composition is based on an engraving by Dürer, though changes have been made; but it has been enriched by the presence of shadows in the background and the life-like portraits of the Carthusian monks, which give to the painting a naturalistic strength anticipating the seventeenth century. There is thus a dualism typical of this tormented artist, although he succeds here in resolving it in a nobly formal masterpiece of a tense and anguished spirituality. The part in the center with the table, painted in silvery tones, is especially remarkable.

This painting of a mischievous little cherub playing a lute is one of Rosso's youthful works, enlivened by many bright touches. In *Moses Defending the Daughters of Jethro* (c. 1523), one of the noblest works of his maturity, the combination of elements is extremely complex and sophisticated; the figures pile up sculpturally, inwards and upwards at the same time; contrasting elements are interwoven, the faces are reduced to unreal masks, and the color is also abstract but sharp. There are details of surprising modernity, as for example the two women's heads at the upper right.

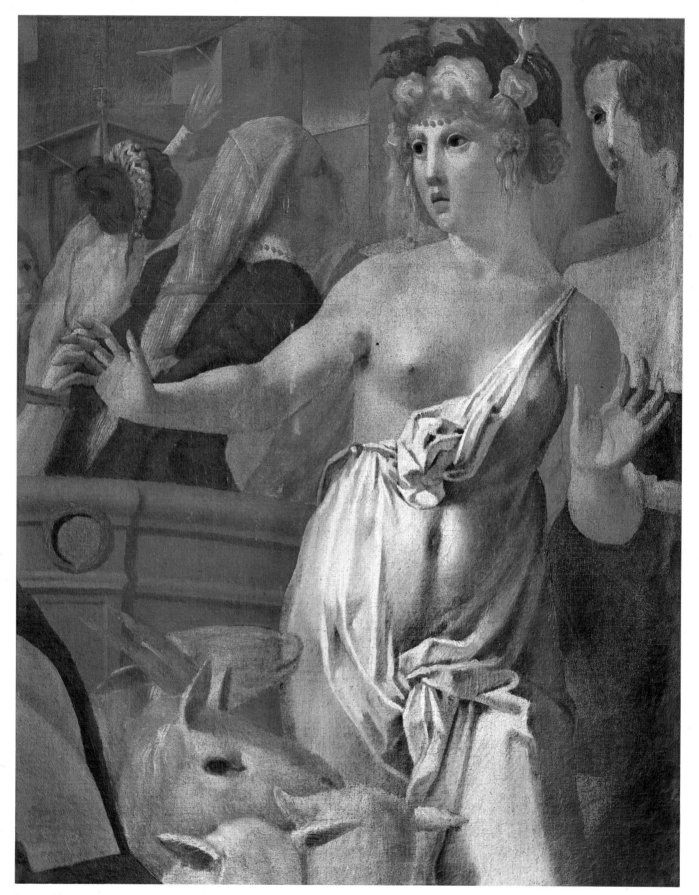

Rosso Fiorentino: Moses Defending the Daughters of Jethro, detail

▲
Vasari: Lorenzo the Magnificent

▶
Bronzino: Portrait of a Girl with Book

The principal heir of Pontormo (who himself painted some extremely fine portraits) was Bronzino (1503-1572). The figures in his portraits are as still and finely wrought as if transformed into colored marble. He painted the city aristocracy and the Medici court, the former — by that time subdued by their Medici rulers — with their covert and unyielding pride, and the latter with the self-assurance that comes of power. *Lucrezia Panciatichi* (whose portrait, together with that of her husband *Bartolomeo*, was painted in about 1540) faces us, emerging from the shadowy background in the glow of her splendid red dress, in a sculptural beauty as closed psychologically as it is severely perfect in form. The portrait of the *Princess Isabella* is more superficial.

Vasari also though inclined to ambitious undertakings carried out in haste, is capable of borrowing from the Florentine ambience the capacities of a good portraitist, as we can see in his painting of *Lorenzo the Magnificent*.

96

Bronzino: Lucrezia Panciatichi

Parmigianino (1503-1540), the leading artist of the Emilian Mannerist school, was trained in the style of Correggio but also absorbed the influence of Raphael as well as, to some extent, that of the Sienese Beccafumi, another of the Tuscan Mannerists, and he was not unaware of the German engravings that circulated at the time. When he was in Rome, between 1525 and 1527, he studied Michelangelo and had contacts with Rosso. In the *Madonna and Saints* at the Uffizi we can see how far the artist had already come from Correggio: the landscape full of Roman ruins no longer seems comfortably familiar, but speaks of sorcery, and the rhythm of the sculptured figures is no longer sweetly graceful but serpentine. There is an air of restlessness in the scene, somberly lit by the setting sun.

But the *Madonna of the Long Neck* which Parmigianino worked on for six years, from 1534 till his death, leaving it not completely finished, shows even more clearly the effect of his early studies; it is on a level with the works of his great Tuscan models, in spite of the difference in structure. The aristocratic and exaggeratedly drawn-out figure of the Virgin is matched by the columns in the background and the amphora carried by the ephebic angel, behind whom the heads of a group of companions, crowded together form a thick intarsia. The body of the Madonna, moreover, is "naked under the tight folds, the Hellenistic ideal, cold as water and as the color of the fabric, enriched by pointed breasts, tapering hands, long toes and locks entwined with elaborate jewels" (Quintavalle). The horizontal line of the Child, in the abandonment of sleep, balances the verticality of the other elements, and its curving rhythm is echoed in the red curtain lifted up on the left. A swift foreshortening of space leads the eye from the foreground into the distance where stands "the prophet terrible as a wax automaton before the steep keyboard of the plinths" (Longhi). We thus have before us a work of extreme preciosity, typically Mannerist in its aspiration to a unique beauty, certainly profane and intellectual rather than religious and spontaneous. We can appreciate how, before the modern critical reappraisal of the Mannerist phenomenon, this work could be rejected for its "affectation and effeminacy"; it was even planned to exchange it for a *Madonna* by Cima da Conegliano in Parma, but this fortunately did not occur.

Parmigianino: Madonna of the Long Neck

97

VENETIAN PAINTING OF THE XVI CENTURY

LORENZO LOTTO (1480-1556)
1. **MADONNA AND CHILD WITH SAINTS**
   (893) Oil on canvas; 0.87 × 0.69.
   Signed and dated 1534.
2. **HEAD OF YOUNG MAN**
   (1481) Oil on wood; 0.28 × 0.23.

DOSSO DOSSI (c. 1489-1542)
3. **PORTRAIT OF A WARRIOR**
   (889) Oil on canvas; 0.85 × 0.70.
4. **WITCHCRAFT**
   (148 P) Oil on canvas; 1.43 × 1.44.
5. **REST ON THE FLIGHT INTO EGYPT**
   (8382) Oil on wood; 0.52 × 0.43.
6. **MADONNA AND CHILD IN GLORY**
   with SS. John the Baptist and John
   the Evangelist
   (7 dep.) Oil on wood; 1.53 × 1.14.

BATTISTA DOSSI (active 1517-1553)
7. **VISION OF ST. ALDEGONDA**
   (1357) Oil on wood; 0.21 × 0.34.

BERNARDINO LICINIO
(active 1511-1549)
8. **MADONNA AND CHILD WITH
   ST. FRANCIS**
   (892) Oil on wood; 0.76 × 1.11.

SEBASTIANO DEL PIOMBO
(c. 1485-1547)
9. **DEATH OF ADONIS**
   (916) Oil on canvas; 1.89 × 2.95.
10. **PORTRAIT OF « LA FORNARINA »**
    (1443) Oil on wood; 0.68 × 0.54.
11. **PORTRAIT OF A MAN (The Sick Man)**
    (2183) Oil on canvas; 0.81 × 0.60.
    Attributed.

PARIS BORDONE (1500-1571)
12. **PORTRAIT OF A MAN**
    (929) Oil on canvas; 1.31 × 1.05.
13. **PORTRAIT OF A MAN IN FURS**
    (907) Oil on canvas; 1.15 × 0.90.

GIOVANNI FRANCESCO CAROTO
(c. 1480-1555)
14. **SLAUGHTER OF THE INNOCENTS**
    (3392) Oil on wood; 1.65 × 1.08.
    Signed.

DOMENICO BRUSASORCI (1494-1567)
15. **BATHSHEBA AT HER BATH**
    (953) Oil on canvas; 1.00 × 1.00.

VENETIAN PAINTING OF THE XVI CENTURY

PAOLO VERONESE (1528-1588)
1. **MARTYRDOM OF ST. JUSTINA**
   (946) Oil on canvas; 1.03 × 1.13.
   Attribuetd.
2. **HOLY FAMILY WITH ST. BARBARA**
   (1433) Oil on canvas; 0.86 × 1.22.
3. **ANNUNCIATION**
   (899) Oil on canvas; 1.43 × 2.91.
4. **ESTHER AND AHASUERUS**
   (912) Oil on canvas; 2.08 × 2.84.
   Attributed.
5. **ST. AGATHA Crowned by Two Angels**
   (1343) Oil on wood; 0.20 × 0.18.

GIOVANNI GIROLAMO SAVOLDO
(c. 1480 - after 1548)
6. **TRANSFIGURATION**
   (930) Oil on wood; 1.41 × 1.26.

GIROLAMO ROMANINO (1485-1566)
7. **PORTRAIT OF A BOY**
   (896) Oil on wood; 0.58 × 0.43.
8. **PORTRAIT OF THEOPHILE FOLENGO**
   (791) Oil on wood; 0.89 × 0.79.

GIOVANNI BATTISTA MORONI
(c. 1519-1578)
9. **PORTRAIT OF UNKNOWN MAN
   WITH BOOK**
   (933) Oil on canvas; 0.69 × 0.61.
10. **PORTRAIT OF GIOVANNI ANTONIO
    PANTERA**
    (941) Oil on canvas; 0.81 × 0.63.
11. **PORTRAIT OF COUNT PIETRO
    SECCO-SUARDO**
    (906) Oil on canvas; 1.83 × 1.02.
    Signed and dated 1563.

GIULIO CAMPI (c. 1501-1572)
12. **PORTRAIT OF ARTIST'S FATHER**
    (1628) Oil on wood; 0.78 × 0.61.
13. **PORTRAIT OF UNKNOWN MAN**
    (1796) Oil on canvas; 0.72 × 0.58.
14. **GUITAR PLAYER**
    (958) Oil on wood; 0.76 × 0.58.

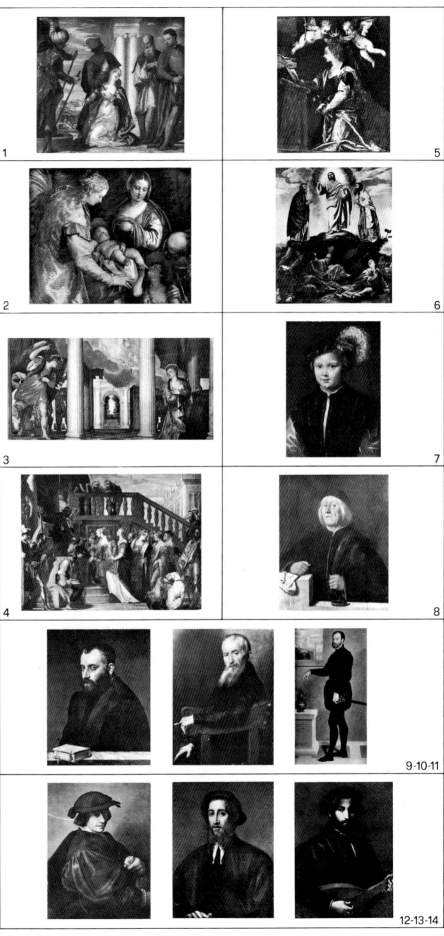

1

2

3

4

5

6

7

8

9-10-11

12-13-14

▶
Dosso Dossi: Witchcraft

▼
Mazzolino: Slaughter of the Innocents

Mannerism became more and more an international phenomenon, diffused both by Italian masters working abroad (Rosso and then Primaticcio and Niccolò dell'Abbate at Fontainebleau, and later Pellegrino Tibaldi in Spain), and by the travels in Italy of northern artists.

Mabuse was in Rome as early as 1508-09, and was "almost the first to take from Italy to Flanders the true manner of making stories full of nude figures and poetry" (Vasari); he was followed by Van Scorel, Heemskerk, Floris, De Vos, Spranger, the German van Aachen, and others. Spain also had early contacts with sixteenth-century Italian painting, in Berruguete, Machuca, Pedro de Campana. The great El Greco also passed through Italy and was profoundly influenced by the experience. Flemish painters, especially, even came down to Italy to stay, for example "Stradano", who worked in Vasari's circle in Florence.

This international Mannerist style, precious and complex, formal but fanciful, intellectual but sensual, is illustrated, within limits, by the Uffizi collections (see the "Corridoio del Cinquecento"). We find, for example, a highly emotive *Christ Carrying the Cross* by the Castilian Luis de Morales. The portrait of *Francis I* by François Clouet (c. 1505-1573), formerly attributed to Holbein, can also be considered a Mannerist painting for its detailed refinement (the rich armor of the King and the sumptuous trappings of the horse), although the formal profile presentation of the subject and the firmness of line are easier to relate to Nordic realism than to the more eclectic taste of the Italian Mannerists. This French king was, in any case, one of the first to show an appreciation of Italian art, and he thus brought about an important change in the national taste.

Clouet: Portrait of Francis I

Ludovico Mazzolino (c. 1479-1528?) continued at Ferrara in the early decades of the new century the tradition of tormented fantasy of the great local fifteenth-century school, absorbing also Nordic influences. The tumultuous scene of the *Slaughter of the Innocents* (of which there is a replica in the Doria Gallery in Rome) was even attributed, in the inventory of the grand ducal collections made in 1704, to Bruegel, because of its bizarre and exotic character; but this can be explained by reference to Ferrarese art in general, with certain influences from Dosso in particular.

Dosso Dossi (c. 1490?-1542) was an innovator, building on his knowledge of the tonal painting of Giorgione and Titian and the formal grandeur of Raphael. He had a warm and sensual imagination, and was particularly gifted in the portrayal of profane subjects and mythological themes, making them extremely evocative.

With its bright colors, and a tactile strength which seems to anticipate certain aspects of the seventeenth century, Dosso's *Witchcraft* in the Uffizi is a late and representative work. Bought in Siena in 1665 by

Cardinal Leopoldo dei Medici, it was described as "the painting with the portraits of the buffoons of the dukes of Ferrara", and it is in fact possible that it came from the "Room of the Alabasters" in the Castle of Ferrara. The subject is unclear, but it probably represents a magical procedure for making the young man in the center, holding the rock, fall in love with the woman near him. The magician would be the semi-naked and garlanded figure on the left, who is touching the glass ball with his rod.

101

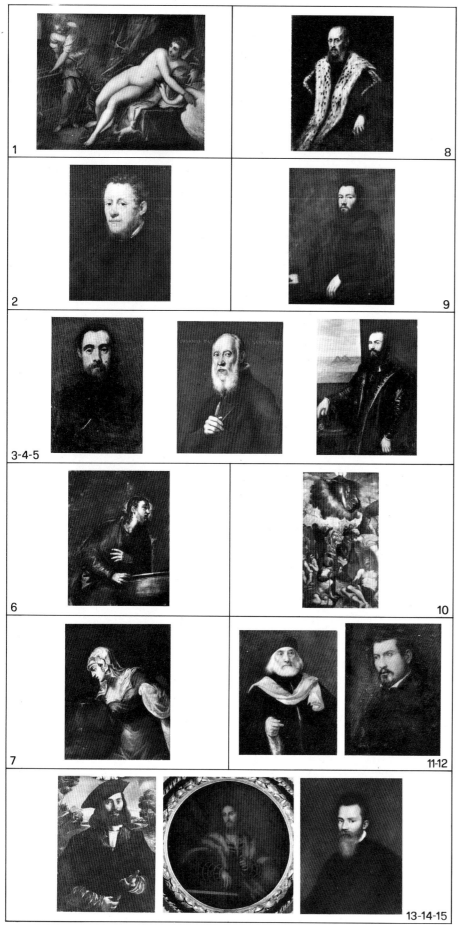

VENETIAN PAINTING OF XVI CENTURY

JACOPO TINTORETTO (1518-1594)
1. **LEDA AND THE SWAN**
   (3084) Oil on canvas; 1.62 × 2.18.
2. **PORTRAIT OF MAN WITH RED HAIR**
   (924) Oil on canvas 0.52 × 0.43.
3. **PORTRAIT OF A MAN**
   (1387) Oil on wood; 0.29 × 0.22.
   Signed and dated 1546.
4. **PORTRAIT OF JACOPO SANSOVINO**
   (957) Oil on canvas; 0.70 × 0.65.
5. **PORTRAIT OF AN ADMIRAL**
   (921) Oil on canvas; 1.27 × 0.99.
6. **CHRIST AT THE WELL**
   (3497) Oil on canvas; 1.16 × 0.93.
7. **THE SAMARITAN WOMAN**
   (3498) Oil on canvas; 1.16 × 0.93.
8. **PORTRAIT OF OLD MAN IN FURS**
   (935) Oil on canvas; 1.12 × 0.88.
9. **PORTRAIT OF GENTLEMAN**
   (966) Oil on canvas; 0.95 × 0.76.
   Attributed.

DOMENICO TINTORETTO (1562-1637)
10. **APPARITION OF ST. AUGUSTINE**
    (914) Oil on canvas; 1.87 × 1.08.

VENETIAN SCHOOL (Second Half of XVI Century)
11. **PORTRAIT OF A SENATOR**
    (2195) Oil on canvas; 0.73 × 0.60.

DOMENICO CAMPAGNOLA
(d. after 1562)
12. **PORTRAIT OF A MAN**
    (895) Oil on canvas; 0.62 × 0.45.

ALESSANDRO OLIVIERO (First Half of XVI Century)
13. **PORTRAIT OF A MAN**
    (1688) Oil on canvas; 0.78 × 0.60.

VENETIAN SCHOOL (XVI Century)
14. **PORTRAIT OF A SURVEYOR**
    (970) Oil on Slate; tondo; diameter: 1.03.

VENETIAN SCHOOL (Second Half of XVI Century)
15. **PORTRAIT OF A MAN**
    (897) Oil on canvas; 0.49 × 0.40.

PAINTING OF THE VENETO AND OF THE COUNTER-REFORMATION

JACOPO BASSANO (c. 1515-1592)
1. **HUNTING DOGS**
   (965) Oil on canvas; 0.85 × 1.26.
2. **THE BURNING BUSH**
   (913) Oil on canvas; 0.96 × 1.69.
3. **PORTRAIT OF AN ARTIST**
   (969) Oil on canvas; 1.08 × 0.87.

LEANDRO BASSANO (1557-1622)
4. **FAMILY CONCERT**
   (915) Oil on canvas; 1.20 × 1.84.

PALMA THE YOUNGER (1544-1628)
5. **ST. MARGARET**
   (928) Oil on canvas; 1.65 × 0.98.

GIROLAMO MUZIANO (1530-1592)
6. **PORTRAIT OF A MAN**
   (891) Oil on canvas; 0.75 × 0.60.

VENETIAN SCHOOL (XVI Century)
7. **HEAD OF OLD MAN**
   (7103) Oil on paper mounted on wood;
   0.56 × 0.39.

FEDERIGO BAROCCI (1528-1612)
8. **PORTRAIT OF A WOMAN**
   (765) Oil on wood; 0.45 × 0.33.
9. **PORTRAIT OF FRANCESCO MARIA DELLA ROVERE**
   (1438) Oil on canvas; 1.13 × 0.93.
10. **MADONNA OF THE PEOPLE**
    (Madonna del Popolo)
    (751) Oil on wood; 3.59 × 2.52.
    Signed.
11. **NOLI ME TANGERE**
    (798) Oil on canvas; 1.22 × 0.91.
12. **ST. FRANCIS RECEIVING THE STIGMATA**
    (790) Oil on canvas; 1.26 × 0.98.

TIBERIO TINELLI (1586-1638)
13. **PORTRAIT OF THE POET GIULIO STROZZI**
    (750) Oil on canvas; 0.83 × 0.64.

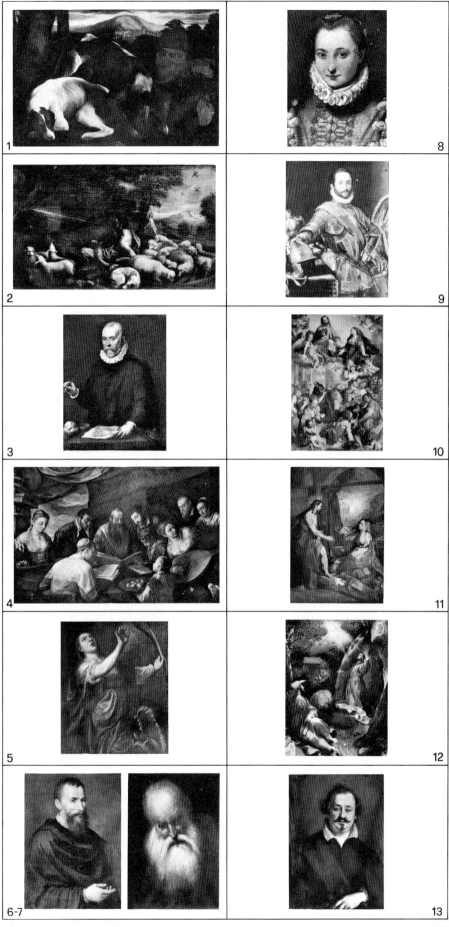

Sebastiano del Piombo (1485-1547) formed his style under the influence of the mature Giorgione and then went to Rome, where he introduced Venetian tonal painting, himself adopting, on the other hand, the monumentalism of Raphael and Michelangelo. He thus plays an important historical rôle, and the fine results of this combination can be seen in the *Death of Adonis* in the Uffizi, where the strongly sculptural and fleshy figures move in slow rhythm in a twilight atmosphere, with a superb and melancholy lagoon landscape in the background.

Venetian coloring combined with Roman formalism, and elements of Manneristic restlessness as well, are found also in the work of Lorenzo Lotto (1480-1556). He worked in various places in the Marches, then in Rome, then Bergamo, and again in Venice and the Marches, always open to new influences, such as the Lombard "realistic" tradition, the teaching of Leonardo and of Titian, and "Expressionistic" German painting. The refined and hypersensitive Lotto succeeded in fusing all of these various elements and producing works of emotional strength and vibrancy, with vivid and lyrical coloring. Observe, in the *Madonna and Child with Saints* (1534) in the Uffizi, the richness of his cool, transparent tones, and the uneasy, eccentric positioning of the figures.

Giovanni Battista Moroni (c. 1520-1578) was from Bergamo, a pupil of the Brescian Moretto, and represents in his portraits the Lombard trend towards realism, quite different, for example, from the courtly and aristocratic portraiture of a Bronzino. At the same time he also, like the Brescians, looked to Venice, striving to recapture the romanticism of Giorgione, Titian's forthright graphic strength, the nobility of Paolo Veronese. In his portrait of *Count Pietro Secco-Suardi*, the architectural background helps to make the black-clothed figure stand out with a restrained eloquence which, however, does not go beyond a faithful and lively representation of both the appearance and the character of the subject. Moroni is already a "bourgeois" portraitist, and depicts, besides gentlemen, professional people and even artisans.

▲
Sebastiano del Piombo: Death of Adonis
◄
Lorenzo Lotto: Madonna and Child with Saints
►
Moroni: Portrait of Count Pietro Secco Suardi

ET QVID VOLO
NISI VT ARDEAT·

M · D · LXIII ·

LUIS DE MORALES (1517? - 1586)
1. **CHRIST CARRYING THE CROSS**
   (3112) Oil on wood; 0.59 × 0.56.

JEAN PERRÉAL (c. 1455-1530)
2. **PORTRAIT OF A WOMAN**
   (37 dep.) Oil on wood; 0.37 × 0.27.
   Attributed.

FRENCH SCHOOL (XVI Century)
3. **PORTRAIT OF CHRISTINE OF LORRAINE**
   (4338) Oil on wood; 0.39 × 0.32.

FRANÇOIS CLOUET (c. 1505-1573)
4. **PORTRAIT OF FRANCIS I OF FRANCE**
   (987) Oil on wood; 0.27 × 0.22.

FRANS POURBUS THE ELDER
(1545-1581)
5. **PORTRAIT OF VIRGILIUS VAN AYTTA**
   (1108) Oil on wood; 0.49 × 0.36.

GEORG PENCZ (c. 1500-1550)
6. **PORTRAIT OF A YOUTH**
   (1891) Oil on wood; 0.91 × 0.70.

MARTEN VAN VALCKENBORCH
(XVI Century)
7. **COUNTRY DANCE**
   (1249) Oil on wood; 0.48 × 0.35.

ANTONIO MORO (ANTHONIS MOR)
(1517-1576)
8. **SELF-PORTRAIT**
   (1637) Oil on wood; 1.13 × 0.87.

CHRISTOPH AMBERGER (c. 1500-1561)
9. **PORTRAIT OF CORNELIUS GROS**
   (1110) Oil on wood; 0.53 × 0.43.

FRENCH SCHOOL (XVI Century)
10. **PORTRAIT OF A WARRIOR**
    (1504) Oil on canvas; 0.70 × 0.57.

ALESSANDRO ALLORI (1535-1607)
11. **PORTRAIT OF A WOMAN**
    (1514) Oil on copper; 0.38 × 0.27.
12. **ALLEGORY OF LIFE (Back of number 11)**
    (1514) Oil on copper; 0.38 × 0.27.
13. **SACRIFICE OF ISAAC**
    (1553) Oil on wood; 0.94 × 1.31.
    Signed and dated 1601.
14. **ST. PETER WALKING ON THE WATER**
    (1549) Oil on copper; 0.47 × 0.40.
    Signed and dated 1606.
15. **PORTRAIT OF TORQUATO TASSO**
    (763) Oil on wood; 0.45 × 0.36.
16. **HERCULES AND THE MUSES**
    (1544) Oil on copper; 0.40 × 0.29.
17. **VENUS AND CUPID**
    (1512) Oil on wood; 0.29 × 0.38.

CORRIDOR OF THE CINQUECENTO

FLEMISH SCHOOL (XVI Century)
1. **HEAD OF MEDUSA**
   (1479) Oil on wood; 0.49 × 0.74.

AGNOLO BRONZINO (1503-1572)
2. **PORTRAIT OF A LADY**
   (793) Oil on wood; 1.21 × 0.96.
3. **PIETÀ**
   (1554) Oil on copper; 0.42 × 0.30.
4. **ALLEGORY OF HAPPINESS**
   (1543) Oil on copper; 0.40 × 0.30.

CECCHINO SALVIATI (1510-1563)
5. **ARTEMESIA WEEPING**
   (1528) Oil on wood; 0.35 × 0.24.
6. **PORTRAIT OF A GENTLEMAN**
   (1581) Oil on wood; 1.00 × 0.77.

ANDREA BOSCOLI (c. 1550-1606)
7. **ST. SEBASTIAN**
   (6204) Oil on wood; 0.48 × 0.26.

JACOPO ZUCCHI (c. 1540 - c. 1590)
8. **THE AGE OF SILVER**
   (1506) Oil on wood; 0.50 × 0.38.
9. **THE AGE OF IRON**
   (1509) Oil on copper; 0.50 × 0.39.
10. **THE AGE OF GOLD**
    (1548) Oil on wood; 0.50 × 0.39.

**FRANCESCO MORANDINI CALLED
IL POPPI** (1544-1584)
11. **THE THREE GRACES**
    (1471) Oil on copper; 0.30 × 0.25.

GREGORIO PAGANI (1558-1605)
12. **JOSEPH AND POTIPHAR'S WIFE**
    (1515) Oil on wood; 0.34 × 0.29.
13. **SUSANNAH AT HER BATH**
    (1511) Oil on wood; 0.34 × 0.29.

GIORGIO VASARI (1511-1574)
14. **VULCAN'S FORGE**
    (1558) Oil on copper; 0.38 × 0.28.

JACOPO LIGOZZI (1543-1627)
15. **FORTUNE**
    (8023) Oil on wood; 0.46 × 0.26.

**JACOPO CHIMENTI CALLED
L'EMPOLI** (c. 1554-1640)
16. **THE DRUNKENNESS OF NOAH**
    (1531) Oil on copper; 0.32 × 0.25.
17. **THE SACRIFICE OF ISAAC**
    (1463) Oil on copper; 0.32 × 0.25.

1

11

2-3-4

5-6-7

8-9-10

12-13-14

15-16-17

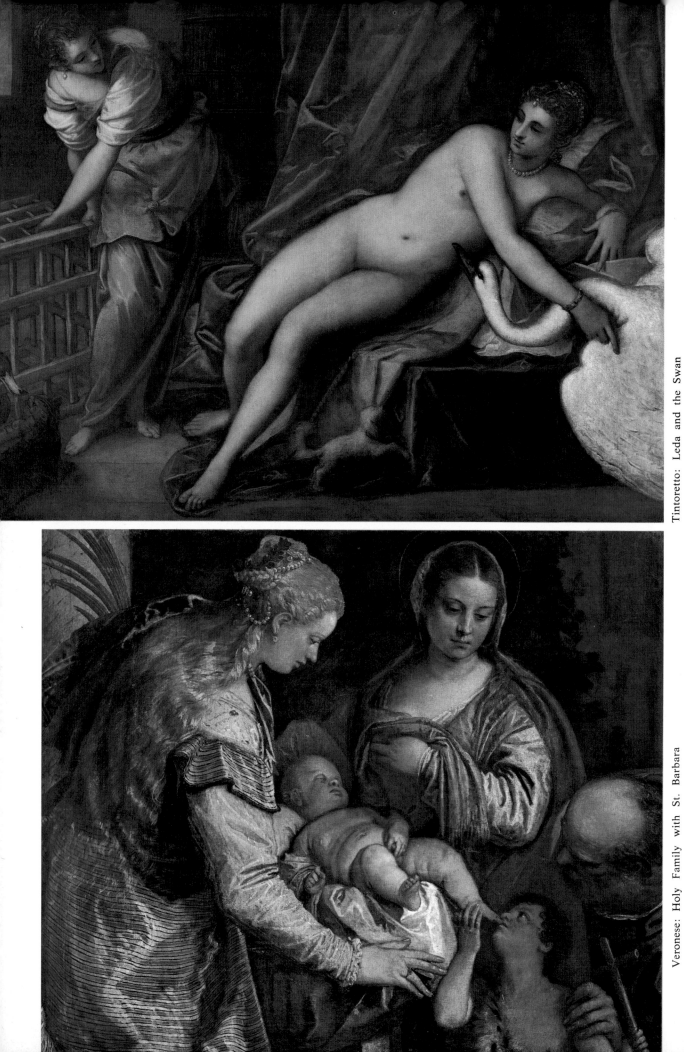

Tintoretto: Leda and the Swan

Veronese: Holy Family with St. Barbara

With Tintoretto (1518-94) Mannerism took hold also of Venetian painting, acording to the formula which the artist himself had chosen: "the drawing of Michelangelo with the coloring of Titian". But in his case the result is quite different from that of Sebastiano del Piombo, who was still bound by a sense of classical moderation. Tintoretto's style is characterized by impetuous immagination and extraordinary rapidity of execution, sinuous modeling combined with sketchy color and contrasting light. His exeptional synthesis of Venetian and Mannerist elements did not fail to puzzle his contemporaries. From the sociological point of view he was among other things, the painter of great canvases for the "Schools", that is, directed to the middle and lower classes, whose religious sensibility he was able to gratify. Professionally, his eagerness to snatch up all possible commissions led to complaints from colleagues (including Paolo Veronese), and his ease of execution made Vasari say of him, "he worked at random and without design, as if to show that this art is a joke...".

In the *Leda* in the Uffizi (a late work, c. 1570) we can note — comparing it, for example, with the *Venus of Titian* — the dynamic structure which, starting from the nude figure, is all in diagonals, and the shadowy atmosphere which makes the scene dramatic as well as sensual and at the same time gives added value to the color tones.

Federico Barocci (1528-1612), from Urbino, inherited the fine sensitivity of Correggio, but expressed it in an ecletic Mannerist style (he also looked to the coloring of the Venetians), and with an obsessive sense of religion dictated by the Counter-Reformation. This *Noli Me Tangere* is signed and dated 1590. It is a sketch for a painting which is now in the Alte Pinakothek in Munich.

Barocci: Noli Me Tangere

Veronese (1528-88) was the rival and in a sense the antithesis of Tintoretto. In place of the dramatic effects and darkly glowing colors of the latter, his works have a rich and serene splendor of classical Mediterranean spirit. His forms, instead of being fused together by color, as was usual in Venetian painting, are sculptural and clearly defined in a limpid atmosphere. He uses complementary tones which create apparent contrasts but add to the luminosity of the effect.

He mirrors in his art the splendors of the sixteenth-century Republic of Venice.

Veronese pursued in this way "the first intent of Art, with a charm and skill never used by any other Painter, for in his Paintings are to be admired pilgrims, majestic Deities, solemn Personages, Matrons full of charms and graces, Royalty dressed in rich apparel, diverse cloths, a variety of military attire, architectural adornments, gay plants, strange animals, and num-

bers of curiosities, which may well satisfy the eye which dwells upon them pleasurably" (Ridolfi).

In the very fine *Holy Family with St. Barbara* (a rather late work) we find all these riches, in the full forms presented with great pictorial skill, in the dense and warm colors. And in the serene nobility of the figures there is also to be found a subtle lyricism and a meditative note particularly evident in the painter's last phase.

ITALIAN AND DUTCH PAINTING OF XVII CENTURY

ANNIBALE CARRACCI (1560-1609)
1. **A BACCHANTE**
   (1452) Oil on canvas; 1.12 × 1.42.
2. **MAN WITH A MONKEY**
   (799) Oil on canvas; 0.68 × 0.59.
3. **PORTRAIT OF A MONK**
   (800) Oil on canvas; 0.66 × 0.54.

GUIDO RENI (1575-1642)
4. **DOMENICAN SAINT**
   (3253) Oil on canvas; 1.15 × 0.86.

FRANCESCO ALBANI (1578-1660)
5. **CUPID'S DANCE**
   (1314) Oil on copper; 0.32 × 0.42.

GUERCINO (1591-1666)
6. **SUMMER DIVERSIONS**
   (1379) Oil on copper; 0.35 × 0.47.

CARAVAGGIO (1573-1610)
7. **YOUNG BACCHUS**
   (5312) Oil on canvas; 0.93 × 0.85.
8. **MEDUSA**
   (1351) Oil on canvas attached to wood;
   diameter: 0.60.
9. **SACRIFICE OF ABRAHAM**
   (4659) Oil on canvas; 1.04 × 1.35.

BATTISTELLO (1570-1637)
10. **SALOME**
    (30 Dep.) Oil on canvas; 1.23 × 1.48.

MATTIA PRETI (1613-1699)
11. **HEALING OF THE OBSESSED**
    (9172) Oil on canvas; 1.35 × 1.18.

BERNARDO CAVALLINO (1622-1654)
12. **ESTHER AND AHASUERUS**
    (6387) Oil on canvas; 0.75 × 1.02

GHERARDO DELLE NOTTI (Gerrit Honthorst) (1590-1656)
13. **A SUPPER**
    (730) Oil on canvas; 1.40 × 2.10.

JACOB VAN RUYSDAEL (1625-1682)
14. **LANDSCAPE**
    (1201) Oil on canvas; 0.52 × 0.60.
    Signed.
15. **LANDSCAPE**
    (8436) Oil on canvas; 0.51 × 0.61.
    Signed.

RUBENS, REMBRANDT AND PORTAITS

PETER PAUL RUBENS (1577-1640)
1. **HENRY IV AT THE BATTLE OF IVRY**
   (722) Oil on canvas; 3.67 × 6.93.
2. **TRIUMPHAL ENTRANCE OF HENRY IV INTO PARIS**
   (729) Oil on canvas; 3.67 × 6.93.
3. **HERCULES BETWEEN VICE AND VIRTUE**
   (1140) Oil on canvas; 1.45 × 1.94.
   Attributed.
4. **TRIUMPHAL ENTRANCE OF FERDINAND OF AUSTRIA INTO ANTWERP**
   (5404) Oil on canvas; 4.04 × 3.28.
5. **BACCHANAL**
   (796) Oil on canvas; 1.52 × 1.18.
   School of Rubens.
6. **PORTRAIT OF ISABELLA BRANDT**
   (779) Oil on wood; 0.86 × 0.62.
7. **PORTRAIT OF PHILIP IV, KING OF SPAIN**
   (792) Oil on canvas; 3.37 × 2.62.
   School of Rubens.

ANTHONY VAN DYCK (1599-1642)
8. **PORTRAIT OF EMPEROR CHARLES V**
   (1439) Oil on canvas; 1.91 × 1.25.

GIOVANNI BATTISTA GAULLI CALLED IL BACICCIO (1639-1709)
9. **PORTRAIT OF CARDINAL LEOPOLDO DE' MEDICI**
   (2194) Oil on canvas; 0.73 × 0.60.

JUSTUS SUSTERMANS (1597-1681)
10. **PORTRAIT OF GALILEO**
    (745) Oil on canvas; 0.66 × 0.56.

ANTHONY VAN DYCK (1599-1642)
11. **PORTRAIT OF GIOVANNI DI MONTFORT**
    (1436) Oil on canvas; 1.22 × 0.89.

REMBRANDT VAN RIJN (1606-1669)
12. **PORTRAIT OF AN OLD MAN**
    (8435) Oil on canvas; 1.02 × 0.73.
13. **SELF-PORTRAIT AS OLD MAN**
    (1871) Oil on canvas; 1.11 × 0.97.
14. **SELF-PORTRAIT AS YOUNG MAN**
    (3890) Oil on canvas; 0.61 × 0.52.

Michelangelo Caravaggio (1573-1610) revolted against much of Italian and European artistic tradition. In his paintings he exchanged idealism for a realism frank almost to the point of brutality. As his contemporary Agucchi said, "Caravaggio, very excellent in his colors, must be compared to Demetrius, because he has left behind the Idea of beauty, ready to follow entirely after likeness". The hierarchy of the genres (in which historical painting came first) was likewise overthrown; "Caravaggio said that it took as much craft for him to make a painting of flowers as of figures". He used plebeian models for his religious paintings, scandalizing many and sometimes causing his patrons to refuse his finished works. But the strength of his true-to-life portrayals aroused also enthusiasm and approval, and an international school formed which looked to him as its head.

Discovered in the storerooms of the Uffizi in 1916-17, the *Bacchus* (c. 1593, painted when the artist was about twenty), is with its luminous clarity typical of his earliest period. The mythical god is represented simply as a soft young boy from the suburbs

Caravaggio: Bacchus

Caravaggio: Sacrifice of Abraham

Caravaggio: Medusa

of Rome, crowned with vine-leaves and holding a goblet of wine. The figure and the still-life formed by the splendid fruit-basket on the table compete equally for attention in this painting, as rich in pictorial substance as it is denuded of traditional content and conventions.

The *Sacrifice of Abraham*, painted some years later, is a more complex composition; in the foreground is the dramatic scene, with a rustic Abraham, a terrified Isaac, and an ambiguously beautiful angel, and beyond it is a spacious sunset landscape, in the Venetian manner. The means of lighting has also changed; some of the luminous parts emerge from shadow, adding strength both to the color values and to the realism of the effect.

Painted on a shield, the *Head of Medusa* (c. 1596-98?) exemplifies a certain tendency to exaggerated cruelty, of thoroughly seventeenth-century and Baroque taste, but undeniably effective, to be found in Caravaggio. The Medusa was originally not among the paintings in the Uffizi, but in the Medici Armory, together with a suit of armor given by the sovereign of Persia, Abbas the Great, to Ferdinando I of Tuscany in 1601.

113

Among the foreign followers of Caravaggio, the Dutchman Gerard Honthorst (1590-1656), who was in Rome from 1615-20, is outstanding. He was nicknamed "Gherardo della Notte" ("of the night") for his preference for candle-lit scenes, and he concentrated on the profane genre. The *Supper with Lute Player* at the Uffizi can probably be identified with the "supper of jolly companions who catch the light from two lamps which flicker and reflect", of which Mancini writes, saying that it was painted "lately for the Serene Lord of Tuscany" (about 1620). Certainly there is a departure here from the dramatic severity of Caravaggio, which has been watered down to create a genre scene of more superficial vivacity. The artist shows great mastery, however, in the play of the lighting, with its golden highlights, and makes fascinating use of color.

Caravaggio's handling of light had an indirect but fertile influence on the vibrant and much more complex painting of Rembrandt van Rijn (1606-69), who also drew on the Venetian colorists in his powerfully romantic and at the same time intimate works. The youthful *Self-Portrait* (c. 1634) belonging to the Uffizi (it came from the collection of the Marchese Gerini) is one of several of this period, which was the painter's happiest also from the personal point of view. The sureness of the construction and the highlighting of certain points contribute to the portrayal of a character essentially proud but also of great sensitiveness. There is also in the Uffizi a *Self-Portrait* from Rembrandt's old age, quite different in its introverted melancholy, and less solid in composition.

Anthony van Dyck (1599-1642) was in substance a disciple of Rubens, but in his works the unrestrained impetuosity of his master was soon toned down, especially when he became, during a stay in Italy (in particular in Genoa, from 1623-27), a portraitist of the aristocracy. When he moved to London (where he lived from 1623 till his death) he took up this speciality again, and represented the British court in figures of subtle and melancholy refinement, with a touch of decadence. The portrait of *Charles V*, a youthful work, was formerly attributed to Rubens himself.

Van Dyck: Portrait of Charles V

▲
Rembrandt: Self-Portrait as a Young Man

◄

Rubens: Isabella Brandt

In 1600 Rubens (1577-1640), who was destined to become the greatest Baroque artist of Northern and Central Europe, came to Italy. He stayed until 1608, in Venice, Mantua, Florence, Rome, Genoa, and during his tour absorbed many influences which were fundamental to his later work. Berenson went so far as to say, "Rubens is an Italian." He studied Titian, Veronese, Tintoretto; Mantegna, Giulio Romano, Raphael, Michelangelo; Barocci, the Florentine Cigoli, the two opposing Roman schools of Caravaggio and the Caracci. He returned to Antwerp already famous, and his career from then on was truly prodigious. He made further journeys, living for a time in Madrid and in London, where he also had diplomatic missions. He painted in all the genres, sacred and historical, landscape and popular scenes, with a creative felicity which combines Classicist eloquence and warm sensuality, lively invention and freshness of tones, sure mastery of his art and deep sincerity. He had an immense influence on Flemish, French, and German painting of the seventeenth century.

The two great canvases in the Uffizi relating to the life of Henry IV of France were painted between 1628 and 1631 for his Queen, Marie dei Medici, to celebrate her consort's victory over the troops of the Catholic League at the *Battle of Ivry* (1590) and his subsequent *Triumphal Entry into Paris.* The life of Marie dei Medici herself had been commemorated by Rubens in a famous series of twenty-one canvases (1621-25), now in the Louvre.

The two paintings in the Uffizi (unfinished) were bought in Antwerp by the Grand Duke Ferdinand II of Tuscany, and came to the Uffizi in 1773. The *Isabella Brandt* of the portrait (previous page) was the painter's first wife. The painting is of about 1620.

Rubens' warmth and grand manner show his debt both to the Venetian masters and to the reformist tendencies of the Bolognese school. Its chief representative was Annibale Caracci (1560-1609), in whose work it achieved a renewed vitality and a Classicist serenity, as we can see in the Titianesque, sensual *Bacchante* in the Uffizi. In the same way, the sensuous painting of Dosso and a reflection of his master Giorgione return in a new seventeenth-century form in the *Summer Diversions* of Guercino, a lively idyll in which the concert of the little party, in the noonday heat, finds echo in the airy and restful landscape.

Rubens: Triumphal Entry into Paris of Henry IV, detail

Guercino: Summer Diversions

Caracci: Bacchante

After the passing of her great sixteenth-century masters Venice became for a time simply the center for painters from other parts, who brought with them the Baroque innovations. Among them were the Genoese Bernardo Strozzi, Domenico Feti, who was trained in Rome in the style of Caravaggio, and the German Jan Lys (c. 1600-1630), who had spent time in Amsterdam, Paris, and Rome and, like Feti had been influenced by Rubens. In Venice Lys broadened his vision, previously restricted to genre subjects of Nordic type, and achieved greater freedom of brushwork, together with a brilliance of color, which in its force anticipates some aspects of the eighteenth century — for example in the *Sacrifice of Isaac* in the Uffizi. In the *Toilet of Venus*, on the other hand, also painted in Venice but earlier, we should note the theatrical Baroque composition and the warm Rubensian sensuality of the nudes.

In the eighteenth century Venice again produced her own great artists, such as G. B. Piazzetta (1638-1754). He was, however, trained in the workshop of Crespi in Bologna, where he learned the "organic distribution of light and shade in pictorial masses". Here too was shaped the fundamental character of his work, "so sensually bound to a frankly popular style", (to quote Pallucchini). The *Susanna and the Elders* in the Uffizi is a youthful work, of before 1720, related to Crespi in the almost coarse sturdiness of the figures and the excited gestures, which are matched by the contrasts of light and the dense, dark coloring. Piazzetta later refined and clarified his style in the best sense of the Venetian tradition. But Crespi's influence remained visible in the lesser but still refined art of Pietro Longhi (1702-86), so akin to the shrewd, good-natured worldliness of the comedies of Goldoni ("Longhi, you who call my Muse sister of your truth-seeking brush"). In Longhi there is perhaps more description for description's sake, an enchantment with rich details, and his slow rhythm seems to reflect that of the gilded decadence of the Most Serene Republic. Our example is the *Confession*, in which the figure of the lady brings a touch of coquettishness into the shadowy and quiet ecclesiastical setting.

▲
Piazzetta: Susanna and the Elders
◄
Lys: Toilet of Venus

Longhi: Confession

With Gian Battista Tiepolo (1696-1770) the long and glorious history of the Venetian school of painting ends in spectacular triumph. He formed his style under the influence of the vigorous relief and burnt chiaroscuro of Piazzetta, and the shadowy effects of Bencovich, but he early showed a tendency to evade realistic limitations and contrasts of light for a broad vision of dynamic and heroic spirit. This quality is already visible in the frescoes in Udine (1726), painted with the collaboration, as regards the perspective, of Mengozzi Colonna, who from then on always worked with him.

Here we find a luminosity and lightness of touch which owe something to the example of the Rococò artist Sebastiano Ricci, in a representation arcadian in tone but at the same time vibrant and powerfully grandiose. Tiepolo painted a great number of works, ever more intense and inventive, both for the ceilings and walls of churches and for secular villas and palaces, working also in Lombardy (at Bergamo, and in palaces in Milan). His style steadily increased in symphonic complexity and in vivacity, carrying to their extreme limit the great Renaissance tradition of Veronese and the Baroque of Pietro da Cortona in richly theatrical compositions or extraordinary representations of vast and dazzlingly lit space, inhabited by crowds of magnificent and happy figures.

From 1750 to 1754 Tiepolo worked in Germany, at Würzburg, creating in the decoration of the Nordic Bishop's Residence a masterpiece of Mediterranean splendor, and in 1762 he was in Madrid, working in the Royal Palace. Here, however, the powers of the last of the great Baroque painters were on the wane. His death, in Madrid, occurred as the colder Neo-Classical style was gaining ground.

The ceiling canvas in the Uffizi (from Udine) representing the *Erection of the Statue of an Emperor*, although a still youthful work (c. 1726) is typical in its brilliant luminosity and vigorous grandeur of Tiepolo's talents. That his paintings should be criticized as rhetorical (as is sometimes done) is absurd, when it is precisely his inexhaustible capacity for fervid and splendid rhetoric that constitutes his genius.

◀

Tiepolo: Erection of the Statue of an Emperor

LANDSCAPE AND GENRE PAINTING

HERCULES SEGHERS (c. 1590 - c. 1640)
1. **LANDSCAPE**
   (1303) Oil on wood; 0.55 × 1.00.

JOHANNES LINGELBACH (1622-1674)
2. **REST AFTER HUNT**
   (1297) Oil on wood; 0.48 × 0.36.

GOTTFRIED SCHALCKEN (1643-1706)
3. **PYGMALION AND GALATEA**
   (1122) Oil on wood; 0.44 × 0.37.

CASPAR NETSCHER (1639-1684)
4. **CLEANING WOMAN**
   (1288) Oil on canvas; 0.31 × 0.23.

CORNELIS BEGA (1620-1664)
5. **GUITAR PLAYER**
   (1187) Oil on wood; 0.36 × 0.32.

GABRIEL METSU (1630-1667)
6. **THE HUNTER AND THE LADY**
   (1296) Oil on wood; 0.58 × 0.43.
   Signed.

FRANS VAN MIERIS (1635-1681)
7. **THE PAINTER'S FAMILY**
   (1306) Oil on wood; 0.52 × 0.40.

RACHELE RUYSCH (1664-1750)
8. **STILL-LIFE-FRUIT**
   (1276) Oil on wood; 0.46 × 0.61.

JAN MIENSE MOLENAER (c. 1610-1668)
9. **PEASANTS AT THE TAVERN**
   (1278) Oil on wood; 0.69 × 1.15.

JAN STEEN (1629-1679)
10. **THE LUNCHEON**
    (1301) Oil on wood; 0.50 × 0.41.
    Signed.

GERRIT BERCKHEYDE (1630-1693)
11. **THE MARKET AT HAARLEM**
    (1219) Oil on canvas; 0.54 × 0.64.

FRANS VAN MIERIS (1635-1681)
12. **THE CHARLATAN**
    (1174) Oil on wood; 0.49 × 0.37.

CORNELIS VAN POELENBURGH
(1586/1590-1667)
13. **LANDSCAPE**
    (1231) Oil on copper; 0.35 × 0.48.

CLAUDE LORRAIN (1600-1682)
14. **PORT WITH VILLA MEDICI**
    (1096) Oil on canvas; 1.02 × 1.33.

▲
Claude Lorrain: Port with Villa Medici

◀
Metsù: The Hunter and the Lady

The collections of seventeenth-century foreign painting in the Uffizi are at present on display only in part for lack of space, but as a whole (including the works now in the storerooms) they are impressive. It was a tradition of the Medici from as far back as the fifteenth century to acquire representative works of the best Northern artists. In the seventeenth century Cosimo II gave hospitality to Callot and Sustermans, and collected landscapes (though these were painted in Rome) by Paul Bril, Elsheimer, Poelenburg. Then Cardinal Giancarlo, the brother of Ferdinando II, who in Rome moved in the circle of Christina of Sweden, met the young Claude Lorrain, of whom he commissioned the very fine *Port with Villa Medici*

(1677). This painting is a masterpiece among the artist's "seaports", combining splendid architectural features, taken from life, with a marvellously effective gilded seascape.

Cardinal Leopoldo, besides the famous collection of self-portraits, collected Flemish and Dutch paintings, while the court commissioned painters of impressive capacity for the imitation of nature, such as Marcellis, who specialized in plants, reptiles and butterflies, and van Aelst, who created magnificent still-lifes. Prince Mattia, a military commander, called to his service the most famous painter of battles of the time, Borgognone.

Cosimo III, ill-treated by historians but a man of undeniable culture, acquired during his youthful travels,

and later through agents, paintings by English, Dutch and Flemish artists, including van Mieris (*Dutch Courtesan*), Dou, van Slingelandt, Netscher, van der Heyden (*View of the Municipal Square of Amsterdam*). It is a pity that Rembrandt had nothing to sell him, and that he bought no Vermeer.

The Ruysdaels were bought in 1797, as part of the additions to the Uffizi which we owe to the good government of the House of Lorraine. As an example of the precise and technically brilliant Dutch taste which impressed Cosimo III we can take the painting by Metsu (1629-67), illustrative and somewhat sentimental.

123

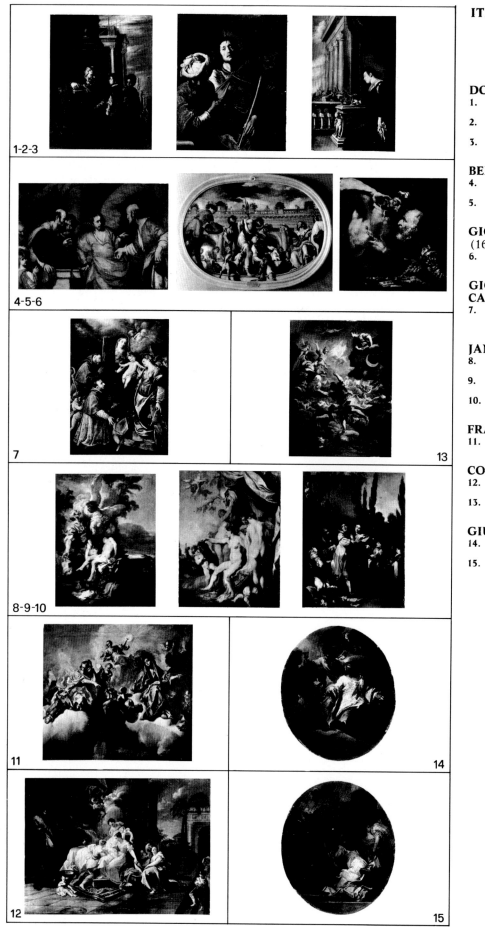

1-2-3

4-5-6

7

13

8-9-10

11

14

12

15

ITALIAN BAROQUE

DOMENICO FETI (c. 1589-1624)
1. **THE FORTUNE TELLER**
   (27 dep.) Oil on canvas; 0.86 × 0.66.
2. **ECCE HOMO**
   (6279) Oil on canvas; 1.37 × 1.13.
3. **ARTEMESIA**
   (1356) Oil on wood; 0.69 × 0.45.

BERNARDO STROZZI (1581-1644)
4. **CHRIST WITH THE PHARISEES**
   (808) Oil on canvas; 1.60 × 2.29.
5. **PARABLE OF THE WEDDING GUEST**
   (2191) Oil on canvas, oval; 1.27 × 1.90.

GIOVANNI BATTISTA LANGETTI
(1625-1676)
6. **CARD PLAYERS**
   (5134) Oil on canvas; 0.96 × 0.96.

**GIOVANNI BATTISTA CRESPI
CALLED IL CERANO** (1576-1632)
7. **MADONNA AND CHILD with SS. Francis,**
   Carlo Borromeo and Catherine
   (3884) Oil on canvas; 2.67 × 2.01.

JAN LYS (d. 1630)
8. **SACRIFICE OF ISAAC**
   (1376) Oil on canvas; 0.88 × 0.70.
9. **TOILET OF VENUS**
   (2179) Oil on canvas; 0.82 × 0.69.
10. **THE PRODIGAL SON**
    (1169) Oil on canvas; 1.15 × 0.93.

FRANCESCO DE MURA (1696-1782)
11. **THEOLOGICAL VIRTUES**
    (6388) Oil on canvas; 1.03 × 0.76.

CORRADO GIAQUINTO (1703 - c. 1765)
12. **BIRTH OF THE VIRGIN**
    (9166) Oil on canvas; 1.03 × 1.72.
13. **ALLEGORY**
    (3234) Oil on canvas; 0.90 × 0.70.

GIUSEPPE BAZZANI (c. 1690-1769)
14. **AGONY IN THE GARDEN**
    (9285) Oval; Oil on canvas; 0.42 × 0.36.
15. **PRESENTATION AT THE TEMPLE**
    (9286) Oval; Oil on canvas; 0.48 × 0.36.

ITALIAN PAINTING OF XVIII CENTURY

ALESSANDRO MAGNASCO
(c. 1667-1747)
1. **GYPSY FAMILY**
   (5053) Oil on canvas; 0.47 × 0.61.
2. **THE PERFORMING CROW**
   (5051) Oil on canvas; 0.47 × 0.61.
3. **THE GYPSY'S MEAL**
   (8470) Oil on canvas; 0.71 × 0.56.
4. **HERMITS IN THE WOODS**
   (5870) Oil on canvas; 0.98 × 0.76.

GIUSEPPE ANGELI (c. 1709-1798)
5. **THE OLD SOLDIER**
   (4701) Oil on canvas; 0.45 × 0.37.
6. **THE PEASANT WOMAN**
   (4700) Oil on canvas; 0.45 × 0.37.

GIOVANNI DOMENICO FERRETTI
(1692-1766)
7. **THE RAPE OF EUROPA**
   (5447) Oil on canvas; 2.05 × 1.46.

GIUSEPPE MARIA CRESPI (1664-1747)
8. **THE FAIR AT POGGIO A CAIANO**
   (26 dep.) Oil on canvas; 1.18 × 1.94.
9. **MASSACRE OF THE INNOCENTS**
   (25 dep.) Oil on canvas; 1.88 × 1.34.
10. **CUPID AND PSYCHE**
    (5443) Oil on canvas; 1.30 × 2.15.
11. **THE ARTIST'S FAMILY**
    (5382) Oil on copper; 0.28 × 0.24.
12. **PASTORAL SCENE**
    (7063) Oil on canvas; 0.50 × 0.38.
    Attribution under discussion.
13. **« THE FLEA »**
    (1408) Oil on copper; 0.28 × 0.24.
14. **THE SINGER AND HER ADMIRERS**
    (6005) Oil on canvas; 0.57 × 0.45.

Canaletto: Ducal Palace

With the eighteenth century, except for the self-portraits, we come to the end of the Uffizi collections. From this century also there are many works at present not exhibited; there is a richly representative collection of Italian artists (Crespi, Piazzetta, Magnasco, Ricci, Pittoni, Pietro and Alessandro Longhi, Canaletto and Bellotto, Guardi, Carriera, De Mura, Giaquinto, and others), as well as some fine foreign pieces. It is worth recalling here that in 1729-93 several seventeenth and eighteenth-century paintings were bought in Paris for the Gallery.

As an example of Venetian landscape painting we reproduce here a typical if not outstanding Canaletto, and a Guardi. The works of Canaletto (1697-1768) are visually exact, almost photographic, excellent in perspective and drawing, quiet but evocative in color. At the same time he is a fine composer of scenes, creating a sense of great animation within a broad framework, and has a seemingly unique sense of town character. His views of England (where he was in 1746) are no less fascinating than the better-known ones of his beloved Venice. Canaletto's fine "prose" contrasts with the "poetry" of Francesco Guardi (1712-1793), with its freedom of imagination and lyrical liveliness of touch. The *Landscape with Canal* is one of his best pieces, fanciful, airy and pictorially acute — with the slender arches of the bridges over the water, and the great Gothic arch that cuts across the steep-roofed building in the background — all in a bluish tone enlivened by silvery lights and a few bright touches of color.

Jean-Etienne Liotard (1702-90) was born in Geneva, trained in Paris, and widely-travelled. He won great fame as a portraitist for his careful, porcelain-like representations, with touches of eccentricity in the dress. The portrait shown here was painted in 1753. Finally, the poetry of the great Chardin (1699-1779), who revived the sixteenth-century Dutch tradition but brought to it a more touching reality, can be seen in this signed painting (bought in 1951), in which the simplicity of the subject is matched by the purity of the pictorial treatment.

▲
Liotard: Princess Marie Adelaide
◄
Guardi: Arch and Seascape
►
Chardin: Boy Playing Cards

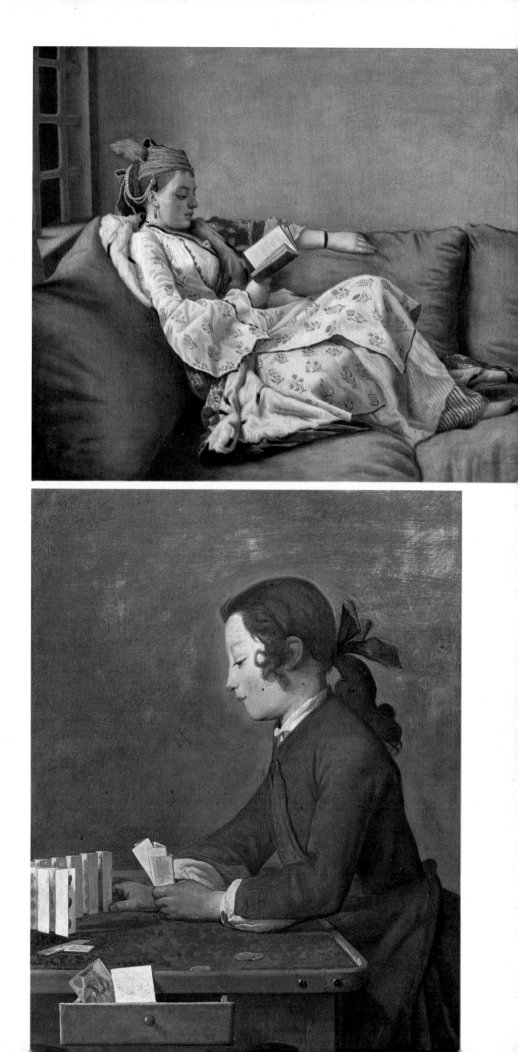

VENETIAN PAINTING OF XVIII CENTURY

POMPEO BATONI (1708-1787)
1. **HERCULES AT THE CROSSROADS**
(8547) Oil on canvas; 0.97 × 0.75.
Lucchese Painter.

SEBASTIANO RICCI (1659-1734)
2. **HERCULES AND CACUS**
(520) Oil on canvas; 0.66 × 0.39.

GIOVANNI BATTISTA PIAZZETTA
(1682-1754)
3. **SUSANNAH AND THE ELDERS**
(8419) Oil on canvas; 1.35 × 1.00.

GIOVANNI BATTISTA TIEPOLO
(1696-1770)
4. **ERECTING A STATUE IN HONOR OF THE EMPEROR**
(3139) Oil on canvas; 4.20 × 1.76.

ROSALBA CARRIERA (1675-1757)
5. **FLORA**
(820) Pastels on paper; 0.46 × 0.33.
6. **PORTRAIT OF AMALIA GIUSEPPA D'ESTE**
(2585) Pastels on paper; 0.54 × 0.42.

ALESSANDRO LONGHI (1733-1813)
7. **PORTRAIT OF A GENTLEWOMAN**
(3573) Oil on canvas; 1.00 × 0.80.
8. **PORTRAIT OF A PRIEST**
(9181) Oil on canvas; 0.94 × 0.78.

PIETRO LONGHI (1702-1785)
9. **CONFESSION**
(9275) Oil on canvas; 0.61 × 0.50.

CANALETTO (1679-1768)
10. **THE DUCAL PALACE AND PIAZZA SAN MARCO**
(1334) Oil on canvas; 0.51 × 0.83.
11. **THE GRAND CANAL AT THE RIALTO BRIDGE**
(1318) Oil on canvas; 0.46 × 0.74.

FRANCESCO GUARDI (1712-1793)
12. **SEASCAPE WITH ARCH**
(3358) Oil on canvas; 0.30 × 0.53.
13. **LANDSCAPE WITH CANAL**
(3359) Oil on canvas; 0.30 × 0.53.

BERNARDO BELLOTTO (1720-1780)
14. **LANDSCAPE WITH RUIN**
(3354) Oil on canvas; 0.46 × 0.60.
15. **VIEW OF THE LAGOON**
(3353) Oil on canvas; 0.46 × 0.60

FRENCH PAINTING

PIERRE MIGNARD (1612-1695)
1. **PORTRAIT OF THE COUNTESS GRIGNAN**
   (989) Oil on canvas; 0.67 × 0.55.

NICOLAS LARGILLIÈRE (1656-1747)
2. **PORTRAIT OF JEAN BAPTISTE ROUSSEAU**
   (997) Oil on canvas; 0.90 × 0.72. Signed and dated 1710.

JEAN GRIMOU (c. 1680-1740)
3. **YOUNG PILGRIM**
   (992) Oil on canvas; 0.81 × 0.63.
4. **YOUNG WOMAN PILGRIM**
   (1016) Oil on canvas; 0.82 × 0.63.

HYACINTE RIGAUD (1659-1743)
5. **PORTRAIT OF BOSSUET**
   (995) Oil on canvas; 0.72 × 0.58. Signed and dated 1693.

ANTOINE WATTEAU (1684-1721)
6. **THE FLUTIST**
   (990) Oil on canvas; 0.36 × 0.46.

JEAN-MARC NATTIER (1685-1776)
7. **PORTRAIT OF MARIE ADELAIDE OF FRANCE AS DIANA**
   (21 dep.) Oil on canvas; 0.94 × 1.28.
8. **PORTRAIT OF MARIE ZEFFERINA OF FRANCE**
   (22 dep.) Oil on canvas; 0.70 × 0.82.
9. **PORTRAIT OF HENRIETTE MARIE OF FRANCE AS FLORA**
   (23 dep.) Oil on canvas; 0.94 × 1.28.

ETIENNE LIOTARD (1702-1789)
10. **PORTRAIT OF MARIE ADELAIDE OF FRANCE**
    (47 dep.) Oil on canvas; 0.57 × 0.48. Dated 1753.

FRANÇOIS BOUCHER (1730-1770)
11. **CHRIST AND JOHN THE BAPTIST AS CHILDREN**
    (976) Oil on canvas; 0.50 × 0.44.

JEAN BAPTISTE SIMEON CHARDIN (1699-1779)
12. **BOY PLAYING CARDS**
    (9273) Oil on canvas; 0.82 × 0.66.
13. **GIRL WITH RACKET AND SHUTTLECOCK**
    (9274) Oil on canvas; 0.82 × 0.66. Signed.

The Vasari Corridor

In 1565 Cosimo I commissioned Vasari to construct him a connecting passage between the Palazzo Vecchio — the seat of the government in the heart of the city — and Palazzo Pitti, the courtly palace on the other side of the river. This project was to be the most ambitious of all the constructions created especially for the celebrations of the wedding of the Prince Regent, Francesco, to Joanna of Austria, in an attempt to give the city the dignity and splendour of a European capital. The story is that Cosimo remembered a passage-way in Troy, which connected the palace of the old Priam with that of Hector — and this was to be paralleled in Florence, with the Regent inhabiting the Palazzo Vecchio and Cosimo the Pitti Palace.

◄

Staircase between the Uffizi and the Vasari Corridor

▲

The Corridor and the Ponte Vecchio seen from the opposite side of the Arno

►

View of the Vasari Corridor

The actual construction of the Corridor was very quick; it was built between the spring and the autumn of 1565. As Vasari wrote: "Five months for a task we did not deem possible in five years". The Corridor begins with the bridge leading from the Palazzo Vecchio to the Uffizi, where it forms part of the Gallery itself; it then leaves the Gallery and, passing over an arcade along the river, joins the Ponte Vecchio, crossing the river. On the other side of the Arno, the Corridor crosses Via de' Bardi and heads towards Palazzo Pitti; in the Square of Santa Felicita it passes along the top of the portico of the church (here the window from which the Grand-Dukes used to attend services has recently been rediscovered). Then, sloping downwards slightly, it reaches the Boboli gardens at almost ground level. Finally, it rises again gently, to join up with the Pitti Palace. Despite its functional simplicity, the Corridor displays architectural style; both in the way the first external part blends with the older architecture of the Ponte Vecchio, and in its internal variety, enhanced by the windows which overlook the river or glimpse up the narrow Florentine streets, or even peer furtively into enclosed gardens and courtyards.

For three centuries the Corridor was set apart for the private use of the reigning family. It was not until 1866 that it was first used for the exhibition of works of art: drawings, prints and tapestries. Later the Iconographical Collection (1200 items) was displayed in this Corridor and stayed here until the last War. During the War the Corridor was used as a means of communication between the partisans and the Allied troops. Its restoration, recently completed by the architect Bemporad, was a labour of many years. In the spring of 1973 the Corridor was re-opened with a new grouping of paintings. It begins with a vast selection of 17th and 18th century paintings; then there are the Italian and foreign self-portraits (415 items), with an interlude near the church of Santa Felicita where there is a display of sketches; finally, a selection from the Iconographical Collection. In all, more than 700 works of art, brought out from the ware-houses in the cellars exhibited over almost two-thirds of a mile.

▲

View of the Ponte Vecchio from a window in the Corridor

◄

View of the Ponte Vecchio and bust of Benvenuto Cellini from a window in the Corridor

132

The Ponte Vecchio

The Collection of Self-portraits was begun by Cardinal Leopoldo de' Medici (1617-1675), and, on his death, together with his other collections, passed into the hands of the Grand-Dukes. The Uffizi actually has in storage a vast number of self-portraits, over a thousand; there are 415 exhibited in the Vasari Corridor, from the Ponte Vecchio to beyond the church of Santa Felicita. They are divided by region and also according to a logical chronological criterion. When you enter, on the right are the Florentines and the Tuscans (naturally the most widely represented), followed by the Romans. On the left the Venetians, the Bolognese and the Neapolitans. It would be impossible to list them all, and it is extremely difficult to point out the more important ones. At the beginning, the self-portrait of Giorgio Vasari, the architect of both the Uffizi and the Corridor, and that of Raphael, painted in Florence, probably in 1506. And then Andrea del Sarto, Bandinelli and Cecchino Salviati. And also Sebastiano Ricci, Rosalba Carriera; Primaticcio, Guido Reni and the Carracci brothers... And Bernini, Pietro da Cortona and Father Andrea Pozzo; and Salvator Rosa and Solimena, the founders of the great Neapolitan school. Finally Pompeo Batoni's beautiful self-portrait.

The background is dominated by the great marble statue of Cardinal Leopoldo, sculpted by Giovanni Battista Foggini, sumptuously baroque in style. These are followed by the self-portraits of foreign painters: Rubens, Rembrandt, then the Flemish and German ones, Zoffany among then; followed by the two self-portraits by Velazquez.

Then Angelica Kauffmann, the French and the English of the 17th and 18th Centuries, Reynolds and More. In the section around Santa Felicita there are both Italians and foreigners painting between the end of the 18th century and the beginning of the 20th. Elizabeth Vigée-Lebrun, Marie Antoinette's favourite painter, Jacques-Louis David, Canova and Mengs. Further on the splendid self-portraits of Delacroix, Corot and Ingres, truly a highpoint of the entire collection.

Agnolo Gaddi: Self-portrait and portraits of Taddeo and Gaddo Gaddi

Francesco Primaticcio: Self-portrait

Cecchino Salviati: Self-portrait

Giovanni Lorenzo Bernini: Self-portrait

Father Andrea Pozzo: Self-portrait

134

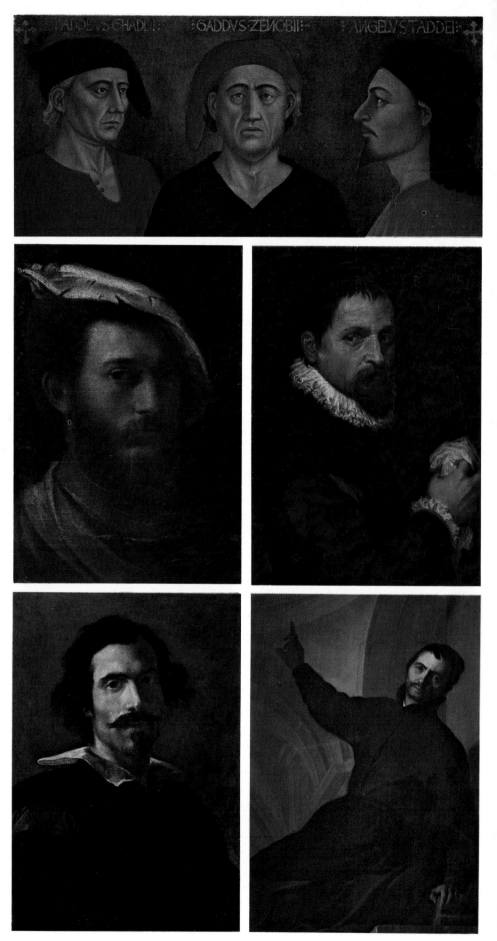

Raphael: Self-portrait

Diego Velazquez: Self-portrait

Rembrandt: Self-portrait

Salvator Rosa: Self-portrait

Angelica Kauffmann: Self-portrait

James More: Self-portrait

Tommaso Minardi: Self-portrait, detail

Joshua Reynolds: Self-portrait

Johann Zoffany: Self-portrait

Anton Raphaël Mengs: Self-portrait

Elisabeth Vigée-Lebrun: Self-portrait

Jean Dominique Ingres: Self-portrait

Jacques-Louis David: Self-portrait

Camille-J.-Baptiste Corot: Self-portrait

Eugène Delacroix: Self-portrait

▶
Arnold Böcklin: Self-portrait

▼
Giovanni Boldini: Self-portrait, detail

▼
James Ensor: Self-portrait

The Iconographical Collection, of which today the Corridor can only exhibit a selection, comprises portraits of the reigning families in any way connected with Florence, such as the Medicis, the Lorraines, the Habsburgs, the Bourbons, etc. It also includes a series of portraits of 'belles dames' of the 16th and 17th Centuries and also other well-known characters of various periods. These works are interesting above all as social documents.

Who were these Medicis, to whom we owe this further collection? If the Medicis of the Renaissance, like Cosimo the Elder or Lorenzo the Magnificent, or even Cosimo I, are universally well-known characters, the later Medicis are much less so. Yet even these last Medicis kept up an atmosphere of intellectual and cultural progress: they were magnanimous in their political dealings and in their patronage of the arts, and, above all, they were passionate collectors. The sickly Cosimo II began the extension of the Pitti Palace in 1620. He was Galileo's patron, and his taste in art was exemplified by the northern schools (Callot and Sustermans). Ferdinando II (d. 1670) succeeded Cosimo II and reigned for half a century. During his reign Florence enjoyed a period of intellectual expansion, assisted also by Ferdinando's brothers, among whom the extremely intelligent Cardinal Leopoldo, a great collector in his own right. It was during this period that the Baroque painter Pietro da Cortona was invited to Florence to decorate the Pitti Palace. Salvator Rosa and Borgognone were both in Florence at this period.

Cosimo III, although bigotted, was still an important patron of the arts; and his son, the Grand Prince Ferdinando, was an interested and cultured patron, who attracted to Florence painters such as Magnasco, Ricci, Crespi. The Last of the Medicis, his brother Gian Gastone (d. 1737), was bizarrely but ingeniously decadent. Even the proud Anna Maria Ludovica, the widow of the Palatine Elector, who died as the last member of the Medici family in 1743, held up the artistic tradition of the family, by ensuring that their collections should remain in Florence forever by the famous agreement established with the Lorraines.

▲
Interior of the Church of Santa Felicita seen from the Vasari Corridor

▶
Giovanni Battista Foggini: Cardinal Leopoldo de' Medici

The Corridor ends in the Boboli gardens, with a first exit near the Buontalenti Grotto (1583-88), a unique place decorated in typically manneristic taste. The Grotto is distinctive for its picturesque façade and for its mosaics and stalactytes.

In the first internal space Michelangelo's four *Prisoners* were placed (now they are at the Accademia and these are merely copies), amidst stone representations of shepherds and animals; the ceiling represents a ruined dome overcome by wild vegetation, and through the open cracks we can see, peering out, animals of different kinds, goats, monkeys, leopards. At one time there was water circulating in tubes in the tree-trunks, which allowed a real maidenhair to grow in the Grotto. In the central tondo of the ceiling there was a crystal ball, full of water and with fish swimming in it. Briefly, the meaning of the Grotto is the continuous change of shapeless matter to matter with form and life (just as Michelangelo's *Prisoners* are still half shapeless stone and already half statues); or, on the other hand, the possibility of ruin or Chaos (the fish in the air), or the return to shapelessness.

In the other two rooms the Grotto was obviously pointing to an erotic meaning, with the *Paris and Helen* by De Rossi and the splendid *Venus stepping out of the bath* by Giambologna, who is lusted after by four fauns hanging on to the bath.

◄
Justus Sustermans: Gian Carlo de' Medici, detail
◄
Anonymous painter, 16th century: Catherine de' Medici
◄
Justus Sustermans: Cosimo II with his wife and son, detail
◄
Giovanna Fratellini: Eleonor of Guastalla, detail
◄
Jan-Frans van Douven: Anna Maria Ludovica with her husband the Elector, detail
◄
Anonymous painter, late 18th century: Portrait of a Lorraine prince, detail
▲
The Buontalenti Grotto in the Boboli gardens
▶
Interior of the Buontalenti Grotto

INDEX

Numbers in dark print indicate color plates

G

H I

J K

L

M